"Marson and Keenan-Miller have put together a respectful, comprehensive, and holistic approach to treating binge eating disorder (BED) which clearly navigates the pitfalls of dieting. By combining science, wisdom, and a broad psychological knowledge base, they gently offer clear, step-by-step guidelines to a healthier and happier you. As a longtime expert in the field of eating disorders, I highly recommend this creative, practical, and user-friendly workbook."

>—**Cyndi Koch, PsyD**, founder and director of The Koch Center, and founder and
>   former director of The Renfrew Center of New Jersey

"Marson and Keenan-Miller offer a way of understanding binge eating disorder that removes the stigma and shame that this illness has previously carried with it. The book is inclusive of all BED sufferers, leaving the reader to feel understood and ready to take action. It holds the attention of the reader with well-thought-out, self-reflective exercises; expert interviews; and tips for making gradual change. As we move away from diet culture and toward a proper mental health lens for understanding binge eating, this book will serve as a manual for overcoming the allure of rigid eating plans and willpower-based interventions."

>—**Heather Russo, LMFT, CEDS-S**, certified supervisor for the International
>   Association of Eating Disorder Professionals

"*The Binge Eating Prevention Workbook* is an outstanding resource and valuable contribution to our field. It is exceptionally well researched, and the material is presented in a clear and relatable manner. Based on their years of clinical experience, Keenan-Miller and Marson truly understand the daily struggles of patients with BED and how to help, and this is evident throughout the book. I look forward to recommending it to patients and colleagues."

>—**Hope W. Levin, MD**, director of psychiatry for UCLA counseling and
>   psychological services

"*The Binge Eating Prevention Workbook* provides an easy-to-follow, comprehensive, and nonjudgmental way to address binge eating in your life. The authors are effective in walking you through realistic, concrete, and achievable ways to successfully move on from binge eating patterns. This workbook will be an excellent addition to my tool kit as a sport psychologist treating eating disorders within the student-athlete population. I highly recommend this workbook for anyone, clinician or not, looking to break down the seemingly ominous task of working through binge eating disorder in a thoughtful and intentional manner."

> —**James Houle, PhD ABPP**, lead sport psychologist for the Ohio State University department of athletics; counseling psychologist specializing in sport psychology and eating disorders; and assistant professor in the department of psychiatry and behavioral health at Ohio State University

"Finally! A practical, clear, step-by-step guide to help reduce binge eating. I am so thrilled to be able to recommend this beautifully written and inspiring workbook to my patients and anyone struggling with compulsive eating."

> —**Leslie Kaplan, MD**, adolescent and young adult medicine expert in the medical care of eating disorders

"It's so rare to find a book that achieves the perfect balance between user-friendliness and hard-core science. Science has the answers, and Marson and Keenan-Miller have deftly turned that science into concrete tasks and activities that anyone can do. This workbook is going to help a lot of people who are stuck in the dieting and bingeing cycle."

> —**A. Janet Tomiyama, PhD**, associate professor of psychology; and director of the dieting, stress, and health laboratory at UCLA

"*The Binge Eating Prevention Workbook* offers the perfect combination of compassion and science. Opportunities for self-reflection and personalized worksheets make this book very engaging, and the best choice for success in overcoming binge eating disorder. Moreover, advice from trusted therapists working with individuals battling BED, and personal insights from those who have recovered, are presented throughout the book—offering real-life application of essential strategies. I applaud the authors for developing a comprehensive and user-friendly workbook that is certain to help so many find peace with food and lasting recovery from BED."

> —**Kathy Isoldi, PhD, RDN, CDN**, associate professor of nutrition at LIU Post in Brookville, NY; and former obesity treatment counselor and coordinator of clinical services at the Comprehensive Weight Control Center at Weill Cornell Medicine in New York, NY

"Lean in… Thank you, Gia and Danielle, for creating a workbook that takes the reader on an eight-week journey to wholeness. With positivity and hope, you 'challenge to change' the reader's relationship with food, self, and others. The interactive chapters, activities, examples, and research are well organized and lead you through with compassion and grace. Thank you for giving us access to this well-stocked toolbox"

> —**Anna Kowalski, MA**, licensed marriage and family therapist, certified eating disorder specialist, and former chief experience officer of Monte Nido and Affiliates

"As owner of a residential treatment center working with teenagers, I have found that resources such as Marson and Keenan-Miller's *The Binge Eating Prevention Workbook* serve as invaluable tools for our program and clinical team, who are consistently challenged with treating a variety of diagnoses and symptoms. While our program specifically focuses on mental and emotional health treatment, our adolescent clients often struggle with their relationship to food, maintaining a balanced diet, and committing to healthy living. This workbook will certainly be an indispensable resource for our therapists, clients, and families."

> —**Jeremy Manné**, founder of Pacific Teen Treatmentin Malibu, CA

"An impactful, responsible, smart, compassionate, and personal approach that motivates the reader to be engaged in their own food relationship process, while at the same time acknowledging them as their own expert. All of which provides getting to the root of the daily issues and challenges one deals with concerning binge eating. This book is a rich toolbox of nurturing skills such as visualization techniques and unique goal setting that promotes self-efficacy to lean into life with love and self-acceptance."

> —**Debra Hopkins**, president and founder of the Breaking The Chains Foundation, vice chair of the NEDA Network executive committee, and ACE Health Coach

"An inspiring workbook that helps translate years of clinical practice and research into a personal journey toward success. For those on the road to recovery from binge eating, I highly recommend reading and utilizing *The Binge Eating Prevention Workbook* for a healthier and happier life!"

> —**Aurelia Nattiv, MD**, professor in the departments of family, and orthopaedic surgery division of sports medicine at UCLA; director of the UCLA bone health practice; and associate team physician for UCLA Athletics

"*The Binge Eating Prevention Workbook* is an excellent resource for anyone struggling with binge eating. Marson and Keenan-Miller use a non-diet approach and coach clients to shed the dieting mind-set; teach how to change all-or-nothing and obsessive thinking; and use visualization, mindfulness, radical acceptance, and more to fight back against binge eating. I can't wait to share this excellent resource with my clients!"

> —**Wendy Sterling, MS, RD, CSSD, CEDRD-S**, coauthor of *No Weigh!* and *How to Nourish Your Child Through an Eating Disorder*

The
Binge Eating
Prevention
Workbook

An Eight-Week Individualized
Program to Overcome Compulsive
Eating *and* Make Peace with Food

GIA MARSON, EdD

DANIELLE KEENAN-MILLER, PhD

New Harbinger Publications, Inc.

Publisher's Note

NEW HARBINGER PUBLICATIONS is a registered trademark of New Harbinger Publications, Inc.

New Harbinger Publications is an employee-owned company

Distributed in Canada by Raincoast Books

Cover design by Sara Christian

Acquired by Jennye Garibaldi

Edited by Marisa Solis

FSC
www.fsc.org
MIX
Paper from
responsible sources
FSC® C011935

Library of Congress Cataloging-in-Publication Data

Names: Marson, Gia, author. | Keenan-Miller, Danielle, author. | Costin, Carolyn, author.
Title: The binge eating prevention workbook : an eight-week individualized program to overcome compulsive eating and make peace with food / Gia Marson, Danielle Keenan-Miller, Carolyn Costin.
Description: Oakland : New Harbinger Publications, [2020] | Includes bibliographical references.
Identifiers: LCCN 2019058724 (print) | LCCN 2019058725 (ebook) | ISBN 9781684033614 (paperback) | ISBN 9781684033621 (pdf) | ISBN 9781684033638 (epub)
Subjects: LCSH: Compulsive eating--Popular works. | Eating disorders--Patients--Rehabilitation. | Eating disorders--Treatment--Popular works.
Classification: LCC RC552.C65 M23 2020 (print) | LCC RC552.C65 (ebook) | DDC 616.85/26--dc23
LC record available at https://lccn.loc.gov/2019058724
LC ebook record available at https://lccn.loc.gov/2019058725

Printed in the United States of America

25   24   23

10   9   8   7   6   5

Contents

Foreword

As a therapist, educator, and author in the eating disorder field, I welcome the addition that Gia Marson and Danielle Keenan-Miller have provided with *The Binge Eating Prevention Workbook*. This book speaks directly to anyone suffering from binge eating, helping them personalize the problem and identify factors that keep them stuck in the binge cycle. Marson and Keenan-Miller maintain a positive tone throughout the book, providing research—along with case examples from people who have recovered—to back up their message that overcoming binge eating is possible.

There are some messages in the book that may be familiar, such as the notions that dieting contributes to binge eating, that thoughts and emotions can affect urges to binge, and that environmental cues and relationship issues can trigger a binge. However, the workbook style—with self-assessments to take and action plans to write out and commit to—help take the material from the abstract to concrete, doable steps. For example, the chapter on setting goals clearly delineates the best way to write goals and structure the process in order to achieve success.

By weaving in the science and describing research studies, the authors wisely help people who binge eat understand why they might behave the way they do around food, creating a pathway to reduce shame and instill hope. Furthermore, they provide specific guidance in a variety of categories that affect binge eating behavior, such as how to change one's thinking, deal with emotions, and improve relationships. A special section on visualization and a chapter on mindfulness explain how making internal changes can alter the course of ingrained, habitual patterns and behaviors.

By the end of the book, those struggling with binge eating will have had practice setting goals and trying out various strategies, which will help in the final task of building their own Binge Eating Prevention Plan. This plan can be used alone or in conjunction with a professional who can help assist in your recovery journey.

Marson and Keenan-Miller pack a lot of material into this user-friendly format, offering useful tools for those suffering from binge eating. *The Binge Eating Prevention Workbook* is a welcome resource for those trying to understand and heal their binge eating as well as those trying to support them.

—Carolyn Costin, LMFT
The Carolyn Costin Institute; Author of *8 Keys to Recovery from an Eating Disorder, The Eating Disorder Sourcebook, 100 Questions and Answers About Eating Disorders, Your Dieting Daughter*, and *Yoga and Eating Disorders*

CHAPTER 1

The Building Blocks of Success

"The journey of a thousand miles begins with a single step."

—Lao-tzu

If you're reading this book, you likely sense that your eating is getting in the way of your happiness. Perhaps you've been told by a doctor, nutritionist, or therapist that you have *binge eating disorder* (*BED*). Or maybe you're uncertain of whether you have a disorder, but you know that you want your eating patterns to change. You might have the sense that your eating is driven by something other than hunger: sadness, anger, habit, or desperation, perhaps. This may be the first time you've ever considered that this problem is not just a failure of willpower.

Regardless of how you think about your eating, you're tired of being at war with food. You're tired of the secrecy and guilt that comes from hiding your overeating from others. You want control over your eating and to return to a place where food is a source of nourishment and enjoyment. If any of this resonates with you, then this book is for you.

First, know that you are not alone. Binge eating disorder is the most common eating disorder in the United States, affecting 3.5 percent of adult women and 2 percent of adult men (Hudson et al. 2007), and about 1 percent of adolescent males and 2 percent of adolescent females (Swanson et al. 2011). Many more people—this might include you—also binge eat but don't meet all of the criteria for the disorder. In fact, most who binge eat don't fit the stereotype of someone with an "eating disorder"—those we tend to think of as young women who have gotten too thin. Because of this perception, many people are surprised to learn that overeating can stem from a true medical condition.

BED is more common than anorexia and bulimia combined, but those disorders get a lot more attention from scientists and the media. That has left many people who binge eat feeling alone, ashamed, and hopeless. But there is reason to be hopeful: Recent advancements in psychological science have taught us that binge eating can be treated successfully using research-tested techniques. And studies have shown that treatment can be just as effective when delivered through a self-help book (Vocks et al. 2010), exactly like the one you're holding. In this book, you will learn the secrets of cutting-edge psychological science so that you can end your binge eating for good.

What Is Binge Eating Disorder?

One of the trickiest parts of overcoming binge eating is recognizing the problem in the first place. It might feel like a long time since you could trust your eating to be "normal." Or maybe you feel as if you've never eaten quite normally, as if you've never been able to trust your hunger and your gut to lead you in the right direction. And in this world of "clean" eating, #cheatmeal posts on social media, constant media coverage of obesity, and a never-ending parade of new diets, it can be hard to know what normal eating looks like.

As you'll learn, there are no strict calorie cutoffs or specific foods that make eating a binge. Instead, the definition of binge eating depends a lot on the way that you feel in response to your eating patterns and the problems that eating causes in your life.

Take a moment now to write out what you see as the current problems with your eating patterns. Also, jot down what you hope will change by completing this workbook.

_____

_____

_____

_____

_____

_____

_____

In psychology research, binge eating episodes are defined as *periods in which someone eats an amount of food that is significantly larger than would be eaten by other people in similar circumstances*. Although many people may feel like they "binged" if they ate an extra slice of pizza or didn't stick to their diet, true binge eating is more extreme than that. It might look like the equivalent of eating several meals' worth of food at one time. It also needs to be more than others would eat in a similar circumstance, so eating a large amount after fasting for a medical test or on Thanksgiving probably doesn't count.

Although many people binge eat from time to time without it having significant consequences on their life, others find that these binge episodes become frequent and start to interfere with their happiness, their relationships, or their sense of self-worth. That's generally when psychologists think that overeating may have crossed into binge eating disorder.

An important part of BED is the sense of losing control over eating. Some people describe it as though someone or something else has taken over; some part of them knows that they should stop eating, but they're not able to. Others describe themselves as zoned out or on autopilot. Many people find that they eat much more quickly than normal and that they eat well beyond the point of fullness and into a place of physical discomfort. Eating during binges may not feel like a conscious choice or a pleasurable indulgence—instead it can feel numb, punishing, or mechanical. That loss of control can be a scary feeling, and it can sometimes contribute to the sense that nothing can be done to stop the pattern of binge eating. The good news is that there are ways to get control *before* and *during* the binge, and you'll learn those in this book.

Binge eating disorder also involves other negative emotions around eating. One common sign of BED is a desire to eat alone due to embarrassment. People with BED often feel that they have to hide their eating, especially their binges, from friends, roommates, family, and romantic partners. They may go to great lengths to hide their binges even from store clerks, buying food at several places to avoid being seen with a large quantity of food. Others describe sneaking out at night to replace food they binged on so that roommates don't notice how much food has gone missing. Following the binge eating episode, people may feel remorse, disgust, or depression. There's often a promise to never binge again, to diet, or to avoid any foods that might trigger a binge. However, those promises don't work and, as you'll learn in this book, can make binge eating worse.

Look at this list of signs and symptoms of BED (American Psychiatric Association 2013) and check any that apply to you:

☐ I eat an amount of food in a two-hour period time that is definitely larger than what most people would eat.*

☐ I feel out of control during binges.*

☐ I eat more rapidly than normal during binges.

☐ I eat until uncomfortably full during binges.

☐ I sometimes binge eat large amounts of food even though I am not feeling physically hungry.

☐ I try to avoid eating around other people.

☐ I avoid social situations based on my eating behaviors or fears.

☐ I feel disgusted or guilty after a binge.

☐ I binge eat at least once most weeks.*

If you checked all three starred items and at least three others, it's likely you meet the diagnostic criteria for binge eating disorder. If you do not meet all of these criteria, however, you may still struggle to eat in a way that promotes your physical and psychological well-being. If you feel as if food has control of you, you can't trust yourself around certain kinds of food, or the way you eat brings pain or shame into your life, that is a serious problem worth treating, regardless of whether you fit all of the criteria for BED. The good news is that the tools in this book can help you to improve your relationship with food, with or without a BED diagnosis.

What Binge Eating Is Not

Take a look at the statements below. Check off any that you have heard from others or that you personally believe to be true:

☐ I should be able to stop binge eating using willpower alone.

☐ If I could just find the right diet and stick to it, I would be able to stop bingeing.

☐ I can't have an eating disorder if I'm not very thin.

☐ I can't have binge eating disorder unless I meet the medical definition of obesity.

☐ I'm weak for letting food have so much control over me.

☐ None of my attempts to stop binge eating have been successful, so I should just give up.

Because binge eating has only been treated as a true disorder by medical professionals since 2013, when it was first described in the official book of psychiatric diagnoses, myths and stigma about the causes and treatments for binge eating are widespread.

Binge eating is *not* a failure of willpower. We know that can be hard to believe. Messages from the media, doctors, and loved ones often imply that binge eating can be stopped by just trying harder to diet and eat healthfully. This myth overlooks the powerful evolutionary, environmental, and biological factors that contribute to binge eating. Our brains are primed to make us overeat, and the mismatch between our ancient, evolutionary brains and the modern, hyper-rich food environment of today makes all of us vulnerable to binge eating. In this book, you'll learn what your specific triggers are and how to overcome them.

Binge eating is *not* curable with a diet. Another powerful myth, maybe one that you've told yourself, is that all it takes to stop binge eating is a highly controlled diet. Perhaps you've tried to avoid carbs, sugar, or your favorite binge foods in hopes of keeping them out of sight and out of mind. Perhaps you've put yourself on a strict diet in an attempt to prevent binge eating. We explore this myth in greater depth in chapter 3, but for now, know that trying to exert more control over your eating is likely to make things *worse* instead of better. That doesn't mean that you should eat anything you want anytime you want—obviously, that won't work either. This book will teach you about the balance between structure and flexibility in eating that will prevent your hunger and your eating from going into hyperdrive.

Binge eating is *not* limited to people at any particular weight. Many people believe that you need to be a certain size or shape to have an eating disorder, but as you learned above, the criteria for BED are not based on weight. Unlike other eating disorders, people with BED may or may not be preoccupied with their weight and shape, but having a lot of body image concerns is associated with additional suffering. Another important distinction from other eating disorders is that people with BED don't intentionally vomit or overexercise following their binges. Those behaviors are more typical among individuals who have bulimia nervosa. If you think your eating problems might be bulimia, we strongly recommend a medical evaluation to check for some of the health consequences that can stem from purging or overexercise.

Binge eating disorder is *not* just about food. It's true that binge eating *involves* food—and changing eating behaviors is clearly an important part of beating binge eating. But binge eating is about a lot more than just food; it's also about emotions, thought patterns, and even relationships. In this book, you'll learn how to change your internal and interpersonal world in a way that supports a healthier relationship to food.

Binge eating is *not* something that's impossible to stop. The truth is, once a person with binge eating seeks out the right science-backed approach to treatment, they can usually get better. It can happen for you. In an early study on the treatment of BED, about half of all of the participants using a self-help book stopped binge eating entirely within twelve weeks (Carter and Fairburn 1998). More recent research suggests that adding in newer techniques to stop binge eating, including mindfulness, can improve treatment outcomes even more. In one recent study, 95 percent of people who completed treatment no longer met criteria for binge eating disorder (Kristeller, Wolever, and Sheets 2014). In fact, a review of more than thirty studies of the treatment of binge eating found that structured self-help books like this one help people to binge less frequently or not at all and to feel better about their bodies and eating patterns, with results equivalent to in-person therapy (Vocks et al. 2010).

We understand that you may feel hopeless, particularly if you've tried again and again without getting anywhere. But this time is going to be different, because you'll have access to the latest scientifically supported tools. Unlike most self-help books that preach a one-size-fits-all approach to overcoming your binge eating, this workbook provides a wide range of tools to help you understand your binge eating at a personal level and stop it in its tracks. Throughout this book, we've included quotes and stories from people who themselves overcame binge eating. Although many of them felt hopeless, frustrated, or overwhelmed at the start, they each achieved success using the strategies we describe here. We consider them experts by experience. Our hope is that their inspirational words will increase your belief in your ability to build your own success story! Let's hear from one of those individuals now.

> "I had read in books and heard from experts that many people fully recover from eating disorders. But I did not believe a total recovery was possible for me. Even after small successes, I knew I would ultimately slip back into my disordered habits. The eating disorder was so much of who I was as a person that I couldn't picture myself without it. I had little, if any, hope for myself...
>
> "So without believing it would work, I just went through the motions. I made changes that I hated and believed that I wouldn't sustain. But I kept making them. Surprisingly, my confidence grew in my ability to break my rituals and be uncomfortable. In time, my thoughts and emotions caught up, and I found myself really wanting to change. The behavior changes came a little easier once I had bought in to the notion that they could help me. But I still 'messed up' often. It was a daily struggle to fight my eating rituals and maintain the behavior changes that I knew were good for me, but every success became a moment I could look to later to remind me of my strength. Eventually, I could go through the motions of healthy eating enough to believe that I could really sustain it...
>
> "I consider myself fully recovered now that my thoughts, emotions, and desires are those of a 'normal,' not food-obsessed person."   —Samuel

How To Use This Book

This book starts with a brief introduction to the causes of binge eating, along with a comprehensive questionnaire designed to help you identify the habits and triggers that are most important in your personal binge eating cycle. You'll learn about the latest science explaining why people binge eat and how they can stop. You will set up a new eating plan—one *not* based on diets or calories—that will help you break free of the cycle of restricting and bingeing.

Armed with knowledge about what has been keeping you stuck in binge eating, you'll move on to an eight-week plan to stop binge eating for good. Each week presents a step-by-step guide to a different scientifically proven strategy for overcoming binge eating. We'll teach you how to *set and visualize goals* that will prevent binges and improve your health. You'll learn why the types of goals you've set in the past, particularly around dieting, might be setting you up for failure.

Written and experiential exercises will help you *transform negative thinking traps* that promote binge eating. The exercises will also invite you to find more effective—and proven—ways to cope with the emotions that contribute to binge eating. In addition, we provide worksheets in this book that are also duplicated online, for your convenience, to download for free any time you wish to access them; you can find them at the website for this book, http://www.newharbinger.com/43614 (see the very back of this book for more details).

You'll also learn about how increasing *mindfulness* can stop a binge eating episode in its tracks. You'll then learn more about how the everyday world we live in sets us up for binge eating and how you can *change your environment* to support your success.

Another key element of the plan is *uncovering your values*, allowing you to meet your deepest needs without relying on binge eating. You'll learn how to *improve the important relationships* in your life—with family, friends, and partners—so that you can fully heal your relationship with food. Each week, you will add a new set of tools to your toolbox.

Finally, the last chapter will lead you through the process of putting together your own personalized and realistic Binge Eating Prevention Plan. *Because there are many factors that lead people to binge eat, there are many paths out of binge eating,* and this section will help you find yours. Using the tools you've discovered throughout this workbook, we'll show you how to put together a step-by-step plan to maximize your success and track your progress. This plan is not a fad or a diet. It is not temporary. It is a sustainable way of relating to food and your body for the rest of your life.

Each of the steps in this book is supported by psychological science, meaning that rigorous scientific studies have shown the positive impact of these techniques and exercises. But we also know from these studies that no technique works for every single person. That's why lots of one-size-fits-all programs for binge eating don't work. *There are many reasons why people binge eat and many effective ways to stop.* Most of us share a tendency to want to skip forward to the parts we think will be most helpful, or we get discouraged if we come across techniques that are difficult. However, the techniques that are going to help you the most may not be obvious, and often the trickiest changes to make are the most important.

To make the best use of the program here, you're going to need to begin an experiment of your own: testing to see what works for you. We encourage you to try out each tool and technique until you find the specific ones that will crack your personal binge eating code. Keep in mind that many of these techniques take practice in order to master, so we suggest trying each one for at least two weeks before you decide if it worked.

Track what you've tried *every week*, noting whether it was successful. If it worked, great! Keep at it! If it partially worked, see if you can modify it to make it even more powerful for you. If it's not successful after two weeks, take an honest look at how you've been applying it. If you've only been trying it in part, maybe revisit it with full effort for one additional week. If you've been applying it faithfully and it still doesn't work for you, put that tool back in the box and pick up the next one.

Keep in mind that some of the ideas that seem the most difficult have the potential to bring the most change, so don't be afraid to step outside of your comfort zone. We hate the phrase "no pain, no gain," but we do believe in "no challenge, no change"! By the end of this program, you're going to have a personalized set of techniques that are matched to your body, mind, and lifestyle, and you're going to finally be free once and for all from binge eating.

Facing the Truth About Binge Eating

Joey Julius's Story

Binge eating disorder often stays hidden from others—and even from yourself. Taking the first step of acknowledging to yourself that your eating patterns are problematic takes insight. Making the decision to get treatment to change those patterns requires determination. Being willing to go public about your disorder and your treatment, particularly when you don't fit the mold of what others might imagine about someone with an eating disorder, takes a special kind of courage. Joey Julius, a Penn State football player who went public about his BED in 2016, exemplifies all of these characteristics (Bieler 2016).

Joey Julius's large frame was a common competitive advantage among collegiate football players, and he was incredibly successful as a kicker also capable of making tremendous tackles. However, his athletic prowess hid an eleven-year battle with food.

As a child, he snuck off to eat large amounts in secrecy, sometimes to the point that he was reeling in pain. In college, he hid his eating disorder by eating healthfully with his teammates and friends, yet binge eating in private. In the spring of 2016, his late-night binges were preventing him from sleeping, taking a toll on his mood and leading to concerning results on physical exams. Joey started to notice that his binge eating was causing feelings of depression and anxiety. When he was finally able to admit his problem to his coaches, they quietly supported him in getting treatment. His coaches and teammates welcomed him back to the team when he was ready.

It took tremendous resolve and determination for Joey to admit the seriousness of his problem and the need for change, even though doing so meant that he could be jeopardizing his position on the team. Even more amazingly, Joey chose to make his diagnosis and treatment public, sharing his story on Facebook in a post that elicited thousands of likes and messages of support. By showing that anyone can have binge eating disorder, Joey has helped to tackle the stigma and misunderstandings around binge eating.

CHAPTER 2

Your Binge Eating Decoder

"Problems are not stop signs, they are guidelines."

—Robert H. Schuller

Binge eating is *not* a failure of willpower. The newest research in the fields of psychology, neuroscience, endocrinology, and nutrition has started to uncover the reasons why some people are prone to binge eating. In this chapter, we share with you the latest studies on the causes of binge eating, which we hope will allow you to gain a new perspective and compassion for yourself. If you're used to blaming your willpower or the power of cookies, the true causes of binge eating might surprise you.

Your binge eating is not a sign that you are weak or haven't tried hard enough. Some factors, like genetics, aren't under your control, but knowing about them can help you stop the cycle of self-blame. Because most of the causes of binge eating are changeable, understanding them will give you some new and more-realistic ideas about modifications you can make in your life to break the bingeing cycle.

"There were so many times I thought—despite all of my effort—that I would never be free of this eating disorder. But now it sometimes feels like a distant memory. Recovery is possible!"
—Hailey

Before you delve into this chapter, we want to acknowledge that you may be yawning at the mention of *science*. Or worried that it will be too difficult to understand. We promise that reading this chapter won't require a degree in biochemistry! On the contrary, we've endeavored to make this chapter as easy to follow as possible. We do so because we believe that a better understanding of BED makes you infinitely better equipped to recognize a binge, see its causes, stop a binge in its tracks, and change your habits for the better over the long term. So try not to skip ahead—remember, *no challenge, no change.*

What Causes Binge Eating?

The current science around binge eating disorder is expansive. The more we learn, the better equipped we are to overcome it. Here is our modest bird's-eye overview of some of the findings about the causes of binge eating.

Genetics and Hormones

Your risk of developing binge eating disorder is higher if someone else in your family has it. Although the home environment may account for part of the reason that binge eating runs in families, careful studies have shown that it's mostly due to genetics. Studies have found that identical twins, who share 100 percent of their genetic code, are much more likely to share binge eating behaviors than fraternal twins, who share only 50 percent of their genetic code, even though both types of twins share a home environment (Mitchell et al. 2010).

Part of the reason that genes can impact eating is because they control hormones like estrogen and progesterone, which are important risk factors for binge eating (Klump et al. 2017). Other research suggests that a particular gene that regulates ghrelin, an appetite-stimulating hormone, is also related to the risk of binge eating (Monteleone et al. 2007).

List any genetic or hormonal factors that might contribute to your binge eating, for example, family members who have or had problems with overeating:

_____

_____

_____

But what does it really mean to say that binge eating is genetic? Are our genes our destiny? Luckily, no. Unlike some medical disorders, such as cystic fibrosis, that are determined entirely by our genes, psychological issues like binge eating are much more complex. Our genes act more like a nudge, one that doesn't have to set you off course as long as you're mindful of it and take active steps to promote your own health. Just because binge eating has a genetic component doesn't mean that you're stuck with it for a lifetime.

Dietary Restriction

One of the most important causes of binge eating, and one of the most essential keys to stopping it, is dietary restriction. That restriction might take the form of a typical diet, such as eating fewer calories in the hopes of losing weight, but as we'll see in chapter 3, there are other subtle forms of psychological restriction that can also cause binges, even if you're eating enough calories overall.

A lot of what we know about the causes of binge eating comes from studies of animals, because it is easy to maintain strict control of their diets and environment (Mathes et al. 2009). We know from these studies that depriving animals of food, even for just a few hours, leads to overeating once the animals have access to food again. That makes sense—all of us have gotten too hungry and then overeaten.

What is more interesting is that these same studies show that animals who were put on a diet in the past and were then allowed to return to their normal weight still showed binge eating behaviors when their diet was over. The likelihood of bingeing is particularly strong for these formerly dieting animals when they're put in stressful environments and in situations where they are allowed access to the animal equivalent of junk food. Because most of us live in stressful environments where foods high in fat and sugar are widely available, it's likely that dieting sets us up for later bingeing.

"I couldn't understand how I could be so disciplined as an athlete but fail to control my eating... [Talking to a health care professional and giving up dieting] helped me to finally understand that it wasn't about a lack of willpower, a quality I knew I had." —Monica Seles, the wildly successful tennis star who spent nine years of her professional career battling binge eating disorder

Studies of human dieting show the same result: dieting increases binge eating. Laboratory studies in which adults have been subjected to highly restrictive diets have shown that people later binge eat once they return to environments with unlimited food (Franklin and Scheile 1948). The same pattern occurs outside of the lab in naturally occurring situations where people are underfed. For example, former prisoners of war who faced chronic food deprivation during captivity were much more likely than non-POW soldiers to show future binge eating, even long after the war was over (Polivy et al. 1994). The same is true for kids and teens. Studies that have tracked children and adolescents over time have found that youth who dieted were more likely to start binge eating over the next one to five years than youth of the same weight who did not diet (Allen et al. 2008; Stice et al. 2008).

Describe any current or past diets that might be contributing to your binge eating:

_____

_____

_____

Among adults with BED, people who eat regularly and don't skip meals have fewer episodes of binge eating (Masheb, Grilo, and White 2011). Therefore, stopping dieting and challenging thoughts around food and weight is one of the most powerful ways to prevent binge eating. This essential step in the recovery process is covered extensively in chapter 3, where you'll learn why diets don't work, detect subtle cues of the diet mindset, and develop a healthy, sustainable eating plan that will free you from the binge eating cycle.

Changes in the Brain

Foods, particularly those high in sugar or fat, activate the reward pathways in the brain. Studies have found that prolonged binge eating can alter the brain's opioid and dopamine pathways, two brain systems that regulate how humans respond to reward (Mathes et al. 2009). This pattern is similar to the changes seen in the brains of people abusing substances, although the changes in response to food are much less strong than those seen in response to drugs. Because of these changes in the reward pathways, the brain may develop patterns that make abstaining from high fat and sugary foods feel unpleasant, driving people to look for some relief by binge eating.

Studies have also found that the brain processes of people with BED can make it more difficult to avoid reacting impulsively, especially around food. In general, people who binge eat show other signs of difficulty resisting impulses, particularly when eating or looking at pictures of food (Schag et al. 2013). For example, women with BED have stronger brain responses to pictures of high-calorie foods than do non–binge eating women of a similar weight (Svaldi, Caffier, and Tuschen-Caffier et al. 2010). These results suggest that the brains of people with BED dedicate more attention to these high-calorie food cues, which makes it more difficult to resist those foods. Studies using advanced brain imaging technology have also found that adults with BED have reduced activity in the parts of the brain that promote self-regulation (Balodis et al. 2013).

List any signs you've noticed of impulsivity in other areas of your life or difficulty turning your attention away from food:

_____

_____

_____

Having a brain that responds in this impulsive way around food makes it much more challenging to exercise positive control when eating. However, there are strategies that you will learn in this book to help your behaviors become driven by your long-term goals rather than your impulses.

Unhelpful Thoughts About Food and Your Body

Many people talk and think in negative ways about their bodies, sometimes with the hope that being self-critical will motivate them to be healthier. However, just the opposite is true: the more negative people are about their body size, weight, or shape, the more likely it is that they will binge eat. Studies that have followed people over time have consistently found that placing a lot of importance on one's weight or shape is a risk factor for starting to binge eat and for worsening binge eating symptoms. That finding holds true across different types of people, including adult men (Dakanalis et al. 2016), teenage girls (Stice, Presnell, and Spangler 2002), and adult women (Grilo 2013).

The negative effects of overvaluing weight and shape hold true regardless of how much someone actually weighs—that is, it's the way you think about your weight, not your weight itself, that determines how severe binge eating gets (Sonneville et al. 2016). Someone who is at a relatively low weight but thinks badly about their own body is at more risk for developing binge eating than someone at a much higher weight who has positive thoughts about their body. Your thoughts about your weight, not the number on the scale, are what set you up for binge eating. That's great news—it means that you can reduce your risk for binge eating just by changing your thoughts.

"I started binge eating at age five for comfort. It's been an off-and-on struggle my whole life. But recovery started when I began to have thoughts that I deserve comfort, peace, joy—a full life. I checked in with these thoughts and kept them in view. On days when I didn't believe the thoughts, I acted as though as I did. Today, I have a relationship with my whole self." —Charlotte

How you think about food can also either help or hurt the quest to quit binge eating. Binges are often preceded by unhelpful thoughts about food—either obsessively thinking about food or trying to totally avoid thinking about food. Defining foods as "bad" versus "good" can also set up people for binge eating by contributing to the diet mindset or encouraging the idea that certain foods are sure to lead to a binge. In fact, just believing that you're not capable of resisting overeating a particular food can perpetuate the binge eating cycle (Glasofer et al. 2013).

Describe any thoughts you have about your body or about food that might be contributing to your binge eating patterns:

_____

_____

_____

Throughout this book, and particularly in Week 3, we'll teach you more helpful and flexible ways to think about food and your body so that you can get out of the cycle of obsessing and instead have a healthier relationship with yourself and the foods you eat.

Emotional Distress

Eating is often as much about emotion as it is about hunger. Positive emotions can be strongly associated with food—think about the role that food plays in cultural celebrations, family gatherings, and parties. Eating is also related to our negative emotions, which is why we call some foods "comfort foods" or talk about "stress eating." Although many people experience some association between their eating and their feelings, that connection appears to be particularly strong—and particularly challenging—in binge eating.

It probably won't surprise you to learn that negative emotions such as sadness, anger, and stress are among the most commonly reported triggers for a binge (Leehr et al. 2015). In fact, women with BED report experiencing a higher level of negative emotions, like being hurt or disappointed, on a daily basis than other women of a similar weight (Zeeck et al. 2011). Those emotions, in turn, are associated with a strong desire to eat, particularly among people who binge eat. This relationship between emotions and eating isn't all in your head—there are real biological reasons it occurs. Stress causes a spike in the release of ghrelin, a hormone that increases hunger (Gluck et al. 2014). In turn, eating foods high in sugar and fat can decrease both biological and psychological measures of stress by activating reward pathways in the brain (Razzoli et al. 2017).

It's not just the amount of stress or emotional upset you're experiencing that impacts your eating; it's also the ways that you cope with those emotions. In general, people who binge eat report more difficulty managing their emotions, and there is a direct correlation between problems regulating emotion and the frequency of binge eating (Kenny, Singleton, and Carter 2017). Some ways of trying to cope with emotions seem particularly problematic; people who rely on avoidance, over-thinking, or fantasizing as ways to deal with negative emotions are more likely to turn to overeating when they are in a bad mood (Spoor et al. 2007). Trying to suppress sad emotions is also associated with a stronger desire to binge eat (Svaldi et al. 2010).

People who binge eat report fear of experiencing negative emotions, and there is some evidence that binge eating is a way of avoiding or reducing negative emotions (Kenardy, Arnow, and Agras 1996). That may seem counterintuitive—most people feel bad about binge eating. However, the guilt after a binge may be easier to tolerate than the depression, anger, or anxiety felt before the binge. In that way, binge eating trades one negative emotion for a different negative emotion that feels less upsetting or easier to control. Even just the process of planning a binge dampens activity in the parts of the brain that process emotion (Pearson et al. 2016).

Take a moment to reflect on the role that emotions play in your personal binge eating patterns:

_____

_____

_____

There are healthy ways to manage emotions of all kinds, and this book—particularly in Week 4—will teach you a variety of tools other than eating that you can use when you're facing stress, sadness, or other negative emotions. It's important to know that negative feelings in binge eating are sometimes a significant concern of their own. About half of people with binge eating disorder have experienced a mood disorder like depression, and a little more than a third have clinically significant levels of anxiety (Grilo, White, and Masheb 2009). If you have a low mood or loss of interest in your usual activities that persists for two weeks, or anxiety that feels hard to control and gets in the way of living your life, it's a good idea to seek professional help from a therapist or doctor. They can assess whether therapy or medication might be helpful.

Interpersonal Problems

One major source of emotional stress, and a common trigger for binge eating, is problems in important relationships. In a large sample of adult women with BED, those who reported having the most interpersonal problems also reported the highest levels of binge eating, preoccupation with weight and shape, and attempts to diet (Ivanova et al. 2015). Specific types of interpersonal problems, particularly around assertiveness and rigidity, are strongly related to binge eating (Blomquist et al. 2012).

On the flip side, having good levels of social support decreases the risk of binge eating. Positive relationships may decrease the risk of low mood, increase our perceptions of being valued and cared for, and help us place less importance on weight and shape. If you're struggling with some of the important relationships in your life, you'll learn ways to improve the quality of those relationships to help you recover from binge eating.

> *"Being able to need things from others, whether they meet that need or not, has freed me of relying only on myself and food for support."* —Samuel

The way that friends and family talk about weight and shape can also be important in the creation and maintenance of binge eating patterns. Adults who binge eat report getting more negative messages from family members in childhood about eating, weight, or body shape (Fairburn et al. 1998). Teasing about weight and shape is also predictive of binge eating because of the negative effects that those kinds of comments have on mood (Womble et al. 2001).

List any relationships that might be contributing to your binge eating:

_____

_____

_____

In Week 6, you'll gain tools to improve your relationships and to communicate effectively with the people around you about how to be helpful in your journey toward recovery.

Habits and Environmental Cues

The modern food environment is also partially to blame for the rise of binge eating. Our brains evolved to have a strong preference for foods high in sugar, fat, and salt (Gearhardt et al. 2011). Those types of foods were scarce in our evolutionary environment, so humans needed to be pretty motivated to seek them out. However, the natural human preference for these calorie-dense foods is being exploited in today's world, as processed foods are designed to contain high levels of these pleasure-inducing properties. These highly processed foods that play on the reward circuitry of the brain can make us want to eat them even if we're not hungry and don't need any more nutrients—thereby divorcing the eating process from the biological needs that have regulated eating over most of human history.

Nonstop exposure to images of high-calorie foods on TV, billboards, and social media also makes it more difficult to control food intake. Particularly in situations when our mind's capacity for self-control is overwhelmed by other factors such as stress, people who are exposed to pictures of high-calorie, low-nutrient foods are more likely to choose those foods and to eat more of them (Hall 2016). In fact, repeatedly eating these foods in a specific environment (like in the car, standing in the kitchen, or at a fast-food spot) might create a habit, such that being back in that environment interrupts the brain's ability to make a more conscious decision about the type and amount of food to eat (Kendig et al. 2016). People with BED are particularly sensitive to cues, like pictures or aromas, that serve as reminders of low-quality foods, and those cues often set off a cycle of craving that leads to binges (Kober and Boswell 2018).

Describe any environmental triggers or habits that make it difficult to stop your cycle of binge eating:

_____

_____

_____

It is possible to make changes to your environment and food selection that will help you to stop the seemingly automatic cycle of binge eating. You'll learn how in week 7.

Binge Eating Decoder

Now is the time to start building your personalized road map out of binge eating. Take the following quiz to identify the factors that are keeping you stuck in the binge cycle. The causes that are most relevant to you are where you'll focus your efforts in the coming chapters. Place a check mark next to each statement that is somewhat or mostly true for you.

Dieting (chapter 3)

☐ I'm on a diet or trying to lose weight.

☐ I have a history of losing and regaining weight.

☐ I don't eat on a regular schedule.

☐ I eat most of my calories in the evening and nighttime.

☐ I have rules for eating, like avoiding eating certain food groups.

☐ I'm dissatisfied with my weight, shape, or size.

Visualizing (chapter 4, week 1)

☐ It's hard for me to imagine what my life would look like without binge eating.

☐ I am not optimistic that I can make lasting change.

☐ I don't believe my imagination has any connection to my actions.

☐ In my mind, all I see are my mistakes. I play failures—the binge episodes—over and over.

☐ I don't know how to mentally plan for success.

☐ My eating is unpredictable. I can't envision it being consistent and intentional.

Goal setting (chapter 5, week 2)

☐ I often give up on my goals after a short period of time.

☐ The goals I set tend to be very ambitious.

☐ It's not always clear to me what steps I need to take in order to achieve my goals.

☐ I tend to adopt the goals of others instead of setting my own goals.

☐ Once I achieve my goals, I have a hard time maintaining them.

☐ I often set goals without really thinking about why I want them.

Thinking (chapter 6, week 3)

☐ I get discouraged when I think that things will never change or get better.

☐ After a binge, I tend to think about myself harshly.

☐ I tend to be pretty black-and-white—things are all good or all bad in my book.

☐ When choosing foods, I often think about what I "should" eat.

☐ Once I have one slipup in my eating or diet habits, it's all over.

☐ I tend to take things pretty personally, even when they might not be totally about me.

Emotions and cravings (chapter 7, week 4)

☐ When I get a strong emotional impulse, I usually follow it.

☐ Others might describe me as hot-tempered or impulsive.

☐ Once I get a particular food on my mind, I find it very difficult not to give in to the craving.

☐ I just can't stand feeling bad or upset.

☐ I get uncomfortable when things are uncertain or out of my control.

☐ Once I start planning a binge, I find it nearly impossible not to go through with it.

Mindfulness (chapter 8, week 5)

☐ I'm often out of touch with the sensations in my body.

☐ I sometimes find that time has slipped away and I'm not sure where it went.

☐ I tend to eat so fast that I don't even taste my food.

☐ If I find myself feeling a negative emotion, I try to distract myself.

☐ My mind feels like it's always running a hundred miles per hour.

☐ I live a lot of my life on autopilot.

Interpersonal connections (chapter 9, week 6)

☐ My eating habits have created problems in my relationships.

☐ I often feel lonely.

☐ I've recently been through a big change in my job, family role, or romantic relationship.

☐ I have a lot of conflict with one of the important people in my life.

☐ When I get stressed out over my relationships, I turn to food.

☐ I don't have people to turn to when I am feeling down.

Environment (chapter 10, week 7)

☐ I see a lot of food on social media.

☐ I have a particular routine for purchasing binge foods.

☐ Most of my evening meals are eaten alone.

☐ I often eat in front of the television or computer.

☐ I can't maintain an exercise habit.

☐ I'm often stressed out.

Values (chapter 11, week 8)

☐ My life feels meaningless or adrift.

☐ I'm often not sure what the right decision is.

☐ I have so much to do that it seems like I never have time to take care of myself.

☐ I find myself trying to "have it all" and then getting burned out.

☐ I often prioritize what other people think is right for me to do.

☐ I rarely consider what is most important to me in life.

Write down the number of check marks you had in each section.

_____ Dieting

_____ Thinking

_____ Interpersonal connections

_____ Goal setting

_____ Emotions and cravings

_____ Environment

_____ Visualizing

_____ Mindfulness

_____ Values

The chapters that correspond with the highest number of check marks are going to be the most important in your personal tool kit for beating binge eating. Each chapter will translate science-based practices into exercises and actions you can take to start making changes. You're going to want to make an extra effort in the chapters you've identified—make completing those exercises a priority, even if they're difficult at first. Remember our motto: no challenge, no change!

What about the chapters for which you had one or zero check marks? First of all, way to go! You're off to a good start in those areas with habits that support healthy eating. We still encourage you to read those chapters, however, because you may find useful information. Regardless of which topics resonate with you, we strongly recommend that you *not* skip chapter 3, because stopping dieting is a crucial step in breaking free of bingeing.

Now that you're an expert on the science of binge eating and have started to identify the types of changes you'll need to make, it's time to move on to the *hows* of change. The exercises in the future chapters will teach you the skills you need to break free of binge eating.

Q&A with Elaine Rosen, MD

David Geffen School of Medicine, UCLA

Should I tell my doctor that I binge eat?

Yes. Binge eating disorder is underdiagnosed and undertreated in primary care settings, even though it is the most common eating disorder. Health care providers may be uncomfortable asking about eating habits and may struggle with how to discuss weight. This discomfort may lead to avoidance of the topic altogether or to attempts to initiate discussions that feel awkward or insensitive. However, an honest dialogue with your provider about binge eating is important for many reasons.

What does my doctor need to know?

That you are interested in knowing about all of your health markers, especially those that may be of concern. With binge eating disorder, you may be at higher risk for a metabolic syndrome and type 2 diabetes. If you prefer not to be weighed at a visit when it's not necessary, ask to skip it. Weight does not always correlate with health. Or you can ask your provider for a "blind" weight—facing away from the number and no one sharing it with you.

How should I start the conversation?

Let your doctor know that you've been diagnosed with binge eating disorder or are dealing with binge eating, how you experience it, and where you are in the recovery process. Ask your doctor to have you sign a release allowing them to collaborate with any members of a multidisciplinary team you might be working with, such as a psychologist and registered dietitian. If you are not comfortable with a question asked of you, let your provider know.

CHAPTER 3

Refuse to Diet—and What to Do Instead

"It isn't the mountain ahead to climb that wears you out;
it is the grain of sand in your shoe."

—Anonymous

The diet mindset is like a grain of sand in your shoe as you try to climb the mountain of beating binge eating. You may hardly know it is there. You may have gotten used to it. You have probably even adapted to it. The discomfort it creates is constant, yet subtle enough that you can ignore it. Despite trying to keep up with food rules, restrictions, and the latest fads, you continue to binge eat.

Dieting will stop you from healing your relationship with food and your body. It will keep you from reaching the top of the mountain.

Now, instead of pushing through the pain, it is time to pause and remove the grain of sand.

Don't worry, we won't take away dieting without giving you something better. You will soon be able to turn your persistence into success.

If you don't diet, good for you. But many people do. And messages about dieting and the promise of weight loss are everywhere in our culture—it's a $66 billion industry that is ready to sell you everything from surgeries to supplements (Sifferlin 2017). Our cultural norms often idealize dieting and weight restriction as part of a "healthy" life. *The problem is that they don't work.* We don't mean that they don't work for you, a conclusion that you may have already come to from repeated and frantic efforts to change your diet or lose weight. We mean that dieting and weight restriction don't work for almost anyone, at least not in the long term. And they definitely do not work while you're recovering from binge eating.

"Dieting was always one of my biggest triggers. It was allowing myself to eat without fear of gaining weight that started my full recovery." —Hailey

In this chapter, we'll do more than tell you not to diet. We'll walk you through building your own eating guidelines and non-binge plan—a central component to your recovery.

What Is Your History with Dieting?

Take a few minutes to reflect on the types of diets you've tried and the frequency.

Have you tried...	Yes or no?	How many times?
Calorie-counting diets		
Low- or no-carb diets (including Atkins)		
Low- or no-sugar diets		
Intermittent fasting or low-fat diets		
Nutrisystem or Weight Watchers diets		
Paleo, ketogenic, or Whole30 diets		
Zone, South Beach, or raw-food diets		
Other:		

Overall, how many times have you dieted? _____

How many of those diets led to permanent, positive changes and no binge eating? _____

Divide the number of successes by your total number of diet attempts. What percentage of your diets have led to sustainable positive changes and no binge eating?

_____

How do you feel about your dieting history?

_____

_____

_____

If you've tried dieting twenty times and had one lasting success, that's a 5 percent chance of using dieting as the method to improve how and what you eat—and to stop binge eating. Since you're reading this book, we know you are highly motivated to make real change and make peace with food. Take a few minutes to reflect on what is motivating you to make these positive changes *now*:

_____

_____

_____

_____

_____

_____

_____

Your change begins here. We will teach you the strategies that are proven to lead to lasting success by tailoring research-backed findings about healthy eating to your lifestyle. If you are dieting, we are going to ask you to give it up so you can be free from binge eating. Giving up dieting and any weight-loss goal is essential to your healing. Let's start with a quick (we promise!) tour of the research on dieting—in case you are still on the fence about giving it up.

More Truths About Dieting

While there is no shortage of companies and individuals who want to sell you on the idea that their product will drastically change your body forever, hardly anyone is honest about the truth—that the vast majority of diets don't work. Not because you're bad or lazy or helpless, but because you're human. In fact, while many people can lose weight in the short term through restrictive dieting, almost all studies of long-term weight loss find that dieting very often backfires.

A study in the UK that followed almost 200,000 higher-weight adults for ten years found that just 1 in 1,290 men and 1 in 677 women obtained a body mass index labeled as normal by their doctors (Fildes et al. 2015). Among people who do manage to lose weight, most regain it (Wing and Phelan 2005). Clearly, most people who try to lose weight will not be able to achieve and sustain that goal in the long run.

Even worse, it seems like dieting not only doesn't work but it can actually *cause you to put on weight.* For example, a fifteen-year study of twins in Finland found that people who went on a diet gained more weight over time than their identical twins who did not diet, even when they started at the same weight (French et al. 1994). In fact, a recent review of dieting research concluded that 7 out of 10 long-term studies found that dieters weighed more than non-dieters; another 2 out of 10 showed no difference, and only 1 found lower weights among dieters (Mann et al. 2007; Pietiläinen et al. 2012).

If you were offered a treatment that had a 1 in 10 chance of improving your condition and a 7 in 10 chance of making it worse, would you take it? What if that treatment also was difficult to do, would raise your level of stress hormones (Tomiyama et al. 2010), and could have serious negative consequences for your overall health?

Our body is set up with a strong and complex set of biological, psychological, and environmental systems that fight against weight loss, becoming desperate to adapt when it's deprived. Often we are tricked into believing in the power of diets because we see *short-term results*, without seeing the *long-term consequences.* A study of fourteen contestants on *The Biggest Loser,* a popular TV show that highlighted extreme weight loss, helps paint a picture of the difficulty of maintaining a lower weight (Fothergill et al. 2016). The study found that six years after losing significant weight during the competition, contestants had regained an average of 70 percent of the weight they had lost. Five of the fourteen had returned to their initial weights or even *higher* weights. Scientific analyses revealed that the former contestants showed signs of metabolic adaptation, meaning that they were burning far fewer calories than other people of the same weight in their daily activities, causing them to regain weight.

The very act of dieting also causes biological stress, which triggers the release of a hormone called cortisol that increases fat storage in the body (Tomiyama et al. 2010). Obviously, that defeats the goal that most people have when they start dieting. Even people who can achieve extreme weight loss find themselves powerless against the deeply ingrained biological mechanisms and environmental challenges that prevent the maintenance of weight loss. *The bottom line: depriving your body of sufficient calories teaches it to hold on to every calorie it can.*

Dieting and Binge Eating: An Endless Cycle

Not only does dieting generally not lead to the desired weight loss, it can play a direct role in the creation of binge eating (Fairburn 2013). We know from laboratory studies on a variety of animals, ranging from rats to humans, that persistent caloric deprivation (a.k.a. a diet) leads to binge eating, particularly on highly palatable, nonessential foods (Hagan 2002; Hagan and Moss 1997). We also know that stress can increase that effect—in one study, a history of being put on a diet combined with a small shock to the foot caused rats to eat twice as much of the food that the researchers called "rat junk food" compared to rats who were given a small shock but had never been placed on a diet (Boggiano et al. 2005). Dieting is unlikely to lead to sustainable weight loss, but it can lead to and perpetuate the cycle of binge eating.

In a 1940s landmark study on food deprivation, psychologist Ancel Keys showed that men without any eating problems who were placed on a strict diet began to obsess about food, and that obsession continued on for years after the study was over (Mann 2015). While this food obsession would be helpful if you were starving on a desert island because it would focus your mind on finding food, it is not helpful when you're trying to beat binge eating. In fact, it makes overcoming binge eating nearly impossible (Wegner 1997). Your brain and body are wired to help you survive—thankfully! So despite your greatest ability to exert willpower on eating, when you are deprived of food, you will be primed to seek out food and to overeat in case a period of deprivation happens again (Mann 2015).

The strict rules of diets also create problems. When those rules are broken, you may give up entirely and binge eat. This all-or-nothing thinking (which you'll learn more about in chapter 6) makes it more likely that you'll swing from under-eating to overeating. You might think that breaking some arbitrary limit on your eating is a failure, which may lead to giving up on healthy eating altogether, then a binge. For example, if you get overly hungry, you might eat five or six cookies rather than the one you had planned. After eating the five or six, you might say to yourself, *Well I already blew it, so I might as well have the whole box and a bag of chips and...* Sound familiar?

In fact, the link between dieting and binge eating is so strong that one of us (Danielle) inadvertently led her cat to binge eating simply by trying to reduce his food intake. When she adopted her beloved Tigger from a neighbor, he was an outdoor cat, getting lots of exercise. He was also an incredibly picky eater, turning up his nose at most cat food, any kind of human food, and seemingly anything that she had just bought in bulk. Sometimes his food bowl was still full when Danielle got home from work.

When Danielle learned that Tigger had a health problem that required him to be kept inside, he started getting less exercise and putting on weight. The vet suggested that he go on a diet. With limited access to the foods he was used to, Tigger started binge eating anything he could get his little paws on. Any cat food would be gone in seconds—sometimes he ate so quickly that he would get sick. In addition, he started eating foods he wasn't given, foods that he never showed interest in prior to his diet: bread, butter, table scraps, and even frozen hash browns. Danielle once caught him eating a plate of cashews!

Fortunately for Tigger, the same methods you're learning work for cats. By increasing his food intake slightly and regularizing his eating patterns so that he didn't go too long between meals, he's back to a healthy eating pattern.

What Is the Diet Mindset?

Regardless of whether you've ever been on a formal diet, we hope you'll press pause on the *dieting mindset* to recover from binge eating. What is the dieting mindset exactly? The dieting mindset is a self-imposed cycle of "shoulds" and deprivation.

You might wonder why it is that a person who eats kosher, fasts on a holiday, or avoids nuts because of an allergy isn't dieting? It's because they don't feel deprived. They've anchored their choices of what and when to eat in personal values or health. This is a key distinction.

What makes *you* feel deprived? This will be different for everyone. We have to warn you—you can't trick your own mind, so be honest. As an example, you might decide to stay away from hot peppers because they upset your stomach; that makes good sense and you probably won't feel deprived. Or you may say that you don't like sweets; if true, you won't feel like you're missing out when you skip sweet treats. However, if you *pretend* you don't enjoy sweets (as a diet strategy), you may only abstain because you think you *should*.

Try to be as straightforward and nonjudgmental as possible about your preferences. If your relationship with food is based on rules and shoulds, you may be living with explicit or hidden deprivation: the diet mindset.

"Ask yourself if you are restricting. Are you telling yourself that you are not going to eat for the rest of the day because it's 4:00 and you've already binged four meals? Are you not eating lunch because you are going to a party tonight and you know you will be at the snack table the whole time? Are you sitting down at a meal and already calculating how much food you are going to leave on your plate? I didn't think I had a problem with restriction. But I realized that as long as I was attempting to set limits for myself, I was still in that diet mindset. It wasn't until I let go of all restrictions that I was actually able to stop bingeing." —Mia

Do You Have the Diet Mindset?

Place a check mark next to statements that describe how you think or act, even if it is only sometimes.

☐ I restrict my amount of food.

☐ I don't eat at least three meals daily.

☐ I avoid certain food groups.

☐ I tell myself what I cannot have or what I should not have.

☐ I get too hungry before eating.

☐ I delay eating despite hunger.

☐ I push off my first meal as late as possible.

☐ I eat most of my day's food after 5 p.m.

☐ I make frequent negative comments about my body.

☐ I compare my body or eating habits to others.

☐ I try to trick my mind about foods I enjoy.

☐ I eat as little as possible during the day but wake up hungry in the middle of the night.

☐ I decide an amount of food should be enough, even if I am unsatisfied.

☐ I restrict eating because I'm embarrassed.

Any of the above can keep you stuck in the deprive-binge or binge eating cycle. Take a few minutes to reflect on the items you checked.

Which behaviors and attitudes are most frequent?

_____

_____

_____

_____

Explain how they cause distress.

_____

_____

_____

_____

What is keeping them going?

_____

_____

_____

_____

If you could wave a magic wand over yourself and have a more natural relationship with food, what would change?

_____

_____

_____

_____

_____

_____

_____

_____

We want you to learn to respond to your body's hunger and fullness cues, enjoy variety, consider what gives you energy and satisfies you, and respect the needs of your body and mind. When you stop dieting, you'll decrease your stress response. We offer you a mindset, tools, and plan so you never deprive your body or binge eat again.

"Learning about the effects of dieting and that there was an alternative was one of the most influential factors in my recovery." —Chloe

Letting Go of Losing Weight

We are all surrounded by endless messages about how to change, fix, improve, and criticize our body. Not surprisingly, these messages are counterproductive to beating binge eating. Research suggests that treatment for binge eating is usually weight neutral, meaning that as you implement this plan to beat binge eating, you will likely not gain or lose weight. Don't fret, you are not losing anything by giving up on weight loss. In a review of ten studies, Dugmore and colleagues (2019) found that weight-neutral approaches to health have been shown to be as effective as weight-loss approaches when the goal was physical, psychological, and behavioral improvements. Rather than focus on weight, challenge yourself to focus on less suffering and a life without binge eating for now.

This book's lessons are rooted in the idea that *healthy bodies come in all shapes and sizes*. We endorse the Health At Every Size approach: a focus on health promotion instead of weight management. The science backs us up here. In a review of randomized controlled studies, people made significant improvements in eating behaviors and self-esteem when they focused on health goals rather than on weight goals (Bacon and Lucy 2011). The key *health* marker—the one that prompted you to read this book—is to stop binge eating. So can you agree to set weight and weighing aside for now?

"Dieting gave me the illusion of self-control and the feeling that I was doing something positive... In reality, no. It led to a vicious cycle of restricting, bingeing, then restricting."
—Victoria

All change starts with a decision. Make the decision to beat binge eating. Choose to care for your body—after all, it is yours for life—and to give up dieting. You can change your eating behaviors and how you think about food to stop the cycle of deprivation. It's time to approach long-held beliefs and behaviors with an open mind.

How do you want to relate to food? Reflect on this question and write a short phrase you can say to yourself.

My new (anti-dieting) food mantra: _____

_____

_____

_____

Example: Diets have not brought me lasting change or freedom from binge eating. I refuse to continue what doesn't work. I choose peace and nourishing my body with food.

What is the relationship you want with your body? Consider not how you want it to look but how you want to treat it. Reflect on this question and write a short phrase you can say to yourself.

My new body mantra: _____

_____

_____

_____

Example: I want to feel good and treat my body well with food, sleep, and exercise.

Are you finding yourself a little anxious about giving up dieting? Try relaxation breathing. With your eyes gently open or closed, take some restorative breaths. While allowing your belly to fill with air, breathe in to the count of 3, pause for 1 count, then breathe out to the count of 5. Repeat this six times while saying your mantras out loud or to yourself. If you have trouble, try picturing a balloon filling up with air inside your stomach as you breathe in and the same balloon deflating as you breathe out.

By practicing your new healthy eating and body thoughts, you'll enhance positive motivation. These new intentional thoughts set the stage for change. You will learn more about the role of thoughts in beating binge eating in chapter 6.

What Meaningful Reward Are You Truly Seeking?

If you're finding it difficult to let go of the goal of losing weight, take some time to consider what you hope to get out of weight loss. Then see if you can achieve that goal in another way—perhaps with broader and longer-term benefits in mind. For example, if you want to lose weight for health reasons, such as to reduce your risk of developing type 2 diabetes, focus on behaviors that promote health, like walking for thirty minutes every day. If you want to lose weight so that you have enough energy to chase after your kids, focus on building stamina with exercise. Maybe you want to lose weight as a means to improving your relationships; if so, brainstorm how to enhance your activities or communications to bring you closer. People of all shapes and sizes have close, meaningful relationships.

Refocusing your energies away from the scale and toward goals that are the most meaningful and sustainable will stop the cycle of discouragement and set you up for lasting change. Can you be curious about what you *really* want out of your life and for yourself? Let's explore.

What meaningful rewards have you been seeking (excluding changes in weight, shape, or size) from past diets, the diet mindset, or from binge eating?

_____

_____

_____

_____

What do these rewards say about who you are and what you value?

_____

_____

_____

_____

Write out an alternative strategy to achieve the two most important rewards you are (or have been) seeking through dieting or weight.

One important reward I am seeking is:	Instead of focusing on dieting or weight to achieve it, I will try:
Another important reward I am seeking is:	Instead of focusing on dieting or weight to achieve it, I will try:

Add a Dash of Self-Compassion

When we feel good about something, we take better care of it. Think about a hairstyle you loved, a brand-new car, a burgeoning friendship—how did you treat these things? Probably with a lot of care, right? We invite you to treat your body with the same kindness and care. This can be hard to do, especially as you give up dieting, so be compassionate with yourself.

Kristin Neff (2020), a self-compassion researcher, offers this advice: "Instead of mercilessly judging and criticizing yourself for various inadequacies or shortcomings, self-compassion means you are kind and understanding when confronted with personal failings—after all, who ever said you were supposed to be perfect?"

As you implement positive changes using our program, change your relationship with your body as well. Be grateful for your body—for its functions, for its imperfect humanness, and for all it has done for you over your lifetime (Neff and Germer 2018). This kind of intrinsic motivation to care for yourself is proven to have the greatest potential to bring lasting change (Pink 2009). This is your only body. Treat it with compassion and acceptance beginning today, especially as you work to make healthy changes.

Have you been taking your body for granted, holding on tightly to criticisms or barely noticing what you appreciate? We all do this. And we all can do less of it. So let's pivot right now. Reflect on something your body has enabled you to achieve or enjoy—something that matters to you:

_____

_____

_____

Making an Eating Plan: Your New Normal

As you start to change your eating to be more predictable and intentional, remember that eating is a natural process. You are wired for survival. That means you—your body and mind—can be trusted to succeed on this journey. We will give you the tools to establish this new healthy normal, but in a sense it is a return to scaffolding that is already built inside you. During the next eight weeks, you'll reconnect with your own internal compass.

Starting well is important. If you are engaging in any dieting, select a day to stop dieting and start normalizing your eating. You will build habits and hope. We understand you may be ambivalent about the change. Ambivalence is to be expected. Even good change can feel bad. But trust us and give this approach a try. We have treated thousands of clients with various eating problems. If you want to heal from binge eating, you cannot be dieting. Dieting promises control but delivers loss of control. Dieting promises weight loss but usually delivers weight gain in the long run. The purpose of this book is to give you non-dieting tools to nourish your body, mind, and relationships.

What does non-dieting look like? It will look however you choose to fill out the eating plan at the end of this chapter. We won't tell you what or how much to eat (that would be a diet!), but we trust that you will be able to identify foods you find satisfying, energizing, and easily available.

During the first week, you will eat three meals and three snacks every day. After one week, you can reduce the number of snacks to two by dropping the morning snack as long as you don't get too hungry by lunch. Consider your dietary needs based on age and activity level. Even if this seems too frequent, we recommend you start here, because eating five to six times a day is the frequency of eating that helps most people reconnect with hunger and fullness cues and stop binge eating.

"I changed my actions, and it started with breakfast. I started eating breakfast every morning. Even when I wasn't hungry, even when I binged the night before, even if I thought I was so fat that I didn't deserve to eat it. I was not always successful, mind you, but then, slowly, I stopped being as hungry at the end of the day. I started craving desserts at night less and less. And when I did crave them, I didn't need to go crazy and binge each time. There is, of course, so much more that goes into it. But it all started with breakfast." —Mia

In addition, non-dieting means keeping your calories above 1,500 a day—if you count calories, though we don't recommend you do (Fairburn 2013). The rationale is to not let yourself get too hungry, because hunger can trigger a binge. Physical hunger is a cue that your body needs more food. If you have been restricting certain types of foods—carbs, sweets, or fats, for example—plan to reintroduce them slowly. If you have been depriving yourself of eating enough food to be truly satisfied, make sure your eating plan includes the amount of food you need to sustain and satisfy yourself.

Be Radically Honest with Yourself

If you must have some chocolate every day or love your Friday night pizza delivery, include those foods in your plan. Also include foods that can sometimes trigger a binge—but do so at a time when you are not eating in secret, when you feel most in control, and when you can most likely stick to one serving. In other words, rather than saying, "I won't eat dessert anymore"—the diet mindset—plan for dessert when you are dining out rather than at home, or eat it at home with a family member.

There may be some foods that you want to avoid for now because they leave you not feeling good or because you know you are at risk of binge eating after even a small portion. Eventually, establish goals to be able to eat all foods, but at first it is okay to leave out one or two foods (but not food groups) as long as you don't feel deprived.

We encourage you to include in your plan all of the foods that you love. However, if you have been a frequent dieter, use caution with foods that are high in both sugar and fat—called "highly palatable foods." In laboratory studies, binge eating resulted when, after a history of restricting, the reintroduced foods were highly palatable foods (Boggiano et al. 2009). So especially if you've dieted in the past, proactively decide on the amount, timing, and frequency of highly palatable foods you choose for now. Plan to eat them with other people around and to allow yourself to truly enjoy them.

Even though psychological or physiological deprivation is often the trigger for binge eating, sometimes it is more accidental. Inadvertently getting too hungry, not having food available due to a lack of planning, or eating a little more than planned can also be triggers. Take the time to plan how, when, and what you will eat using the eating plan at the end of this chapter. You will not need this much structure once you've recovered from binge eating, but it is an effective path for overcoming the deprivation-binge cycle.

While some foods are higher in nutritional value than others, all foods can fit into a normal, healthy eating plan. We recommend that you try to choose mostly whole foods such as fresh apples rather than apple juice, roasted chicken instead of chicken nuggets, baked potatoes instead of potato chips. Your mind and body will register physical hunger and fullness more accurately with whole foods. We don't recommend you exclude any foods or label foods as "good" or "bad"—that would be a diet. What we suggest is that you mostly incorporate foods that bring you satisfaction and sustained energy, and help you notice hunger and fullness. If you're not sure how to conceptualize a meal, refer to *the plate method* (Hamilton 2015), described in the "Q&A with Tracey Engelson, RD" in this chapter. Try to come up with as much variety as possible while making your plan realistic, balanced, and pleasurable.

The purpose is to relate to your body respectfully by nourishing yourself throughout the day, every day. This will calm cortisol surges, ease food obsessions, decrease the deprivation-binge cycle, and bring you closer to stopping binge eating. Right now, frequent food is your medicine. Your body and mind are depending on it.

Guidelines for Non-Diet Eating

Each week, revise your eating plan based on what you're learning about your true eating needs and preferences. Try to stick to it. The most important piece of this plan is that you keep following it, even if you have a binge eating episode. In our experience, most people want to eat less after they binge eat. However, that restarts the deprivation-binge cycle. If you binge one night, start the next morning by eating your normal breakfast at your normal time, even if it *seems* impossible to do so. If you binge eat during the day, return to your planned eating at the next meal or snack. You are retraining your body and mind to trust that satisfying food comes at regular intervals. Eating predictably throughout the day without binge eating will soon be your new normal. Keeping up with your eating plan is an essential part of the program.

- Prepare well for the week. Shop for what you need.

- Plan weekday and weekend schedules.

- Write out meals and snacks.

- Don't skip any meals or snacks. Train yourself to eat earlier in the hunger process, before you are starving.

- Try not to eat in between meals and snacks. This helps your hunger and fullness cues.

- Choose balanced meals but not in a perfectionistic way. Don't leave out entire food groups.

- Make this plan yours. Use "I want to" and "I plan to" language, not "I should," "I have to," or "I can't."

- Own the plan. Don't copy something from a book or blog. Use your own words.

- Listen to your body. For example, if eating a bowl of berries before bed helps you feel satisfied and ready to fall asleep, write that into your plan. If eating more protein helps you feel satisfied for longer, add more. If eating dessert as an afternoon snack during work is satisfying, make it a frequent occurrence.

- Eat slowly. Allow your mind to experience satisfaction.

- If you binge eat, return immediately to your eating plan with your next meal or snack.

- If you binge eat, check your plan to be sure you are having enough at meals and snacks.

- Eat at a table and with others when possible. Don't eat in secret.

Your Action Plan

Make a schedule and menu for this week by completing the My Eating Plan worksheet on the next page. If your weekday and weekend schedules differ significantly, make separate plans. We recommend giving yourself two options per meal so that you can choose what is most satisfying or sounds the best each day. Build in pleasure.

"Planning when and what to eat to not get hungry. Planning to see friends and family to not feel lonely. Planning activities to not feel bored... Planning to be successful helps lead to success!" —Victoria

Maintaining your new, non-diet eating guidelines and plan is a central component to freedom from binge eating. Return to this chapter as often as necessary to review key concepts, adapt your guidelines, or adjust your eating plan. We recommend you make eight copies of the My Eating Plan worksheet—one for each week—or download additional blank worksheets from this book's website: http://www.newharbinger.com/43614. Follow your preferences and include foods that satisfy and energize you. If you prefer a lot of variety, fill out two per week to give yourself four options. On days when breakfast is close to lunch, you can skip the midmorning snack. Plan well, because you don't want to miss any other snacks or meals. Remember to drink enough water throughout the day.

My Eating Plan: Week # _____

The day(s) I will **shop** for the food I need this week:

_____

The day(s) I will **prepare** food for the week:

_____

The day I will **start** my new regular eating: _____

My non-diet eating guidelines are: _____

_____

_____

_____

_____

_____

Weekdays

Meals & Snacks	Time	Option 1	Option 2
Breakfast			
Snack			
Lunch			
Snack			
Dinner			
Snack			

Weekends

Meals & Snacks	Time	Option 1	Option 2
Breakfast			
Snack			
Lunch			
Snack			
Dinner			
Snack			

Example

Below is a version of how someone's plan might look.

Meals & Snacks	Time	Option 1	Option 2
Breakfast	7:30 a.m.	Scrambled eggs with spinach; toast	Oatmeal with walnuts and berries
Snack	10 a.m.	Handful of almonds	String cheese
Lunch	12:30 p.m.	Turkey sandwich with lettuce and tomato; apple	Tuna salad on lettuce with grapes; serving-size bag of chips
Snack	3:00 p.m.	Yogurt (not nonfat) with granola	Peanut butter on a rice cake
Dinner	6:00 p.m.	Veggie burger on a bun; mixed vegetables	Pasta with lentils and broccoli
Snack	9:30 p.m.	Grapes	Ice cream bar

Q&A with Tracey Engelson, RD

As a registered dietician, what are the most common food myths you hear from clients who are trying to stop binge eating?

The most common food myth I hear from my clients is that a strict diet plan to "cleanse" or "detox" will rid themselves of their habit of binge eating. They are ready to try just about anything that promotes itself as a "reset." I explain that a reset is not what is needed but, rather, the opposite of what is generally needed, as any sort of diet mentality or rigid rules needs to be taken off the table to allow for healing.

What is the first change to eating you recommend and what is your rationale for it?

My first change to eating that I recommend is the need to be eating every three to four hours, which allows one's blood sugar to maintain a safe level, thus helping to reduce the urge to binge, especially at night—and to be mindful and incorporate balance in those meals. Additionally, it is insightful to get a list of foods my clients binge on, along with a dietary recall of what they eat during the day. So often, on the recall of foods that my clients binge on, I see a list of "bad" foods that are "not permitted" during the day—and are then abused at night.

I encourage working on the idea of having permission to eat these foods, and I recommend bringing these foods back in appropriate amounts. So much of my work with my clients is breaking down and debunking food rules—such as the idea that foods are "good" or "bad," "clean" or "dirty"—and taking away judgments and values in food. I promote eating food to fuel, for fun, and for enjoyment!

Is stopping binge eating just about self-discipline?

Binge eating is absolutely not about not having self-discipline! Binge eating is often related to emotional experiences, a traumatic experience, learned behaviors (often in childhood), and/or the result of attempting diet after diet. My goal is to wipe out all messages that have inundated my clients with regard to food and to impart the true meaning of food: that food should be used to fuel our bodies, to connect with people, and sometimes appropriately used in response to emotional experiences.

Rather than discussing willpower, discipline, or "shoulds," I concentrate on acceptance. It's okay to have a salad for lunch one day and just as okay to have a burger and fries on another day. Empowering someone with the realization that they can decide to eat any food they choose grants them the opportunity to naturally learn to choose a more balanced way of life. Things become less exciting and less alluring when there are no forbidden foods or rigid rules!

What are your tips for planning meals and snacks to stop binge eating?

My guideline for planning meals is having basic macronutrient exchanges present at each meal. If you use the plate method, your plate should have a vegetable, carbohydrate (I recommend variety—at least 50 percent from whole-grain sources), protein, fat (avocado, oils, chia seeds, flax seeds, or dressing), and a fruit. Snacks should include a protein and/or fat. I try to steer away from protein bars, as they typically do not promote a feeling of fullness—I often see my clients mindlessly grazing on other food to satisfy their hunger after eating a protein bar.

How do you feel about diets?

Diets can be sexy—they sound fun, everyone's doing it, and they offer a quick solution to a long-term problem! Unfortunately, diets don't work! They are a huge industry and will never go away.

I work with my clients on sustainable lifelong changes, not encouraging a "diet" that they will end up going off of in six months or less. Often, people will be told that if they restrict this or that, they can lose weight—and they often will! But what we too often see is that the weight is regained quickly after their "diet" ends—sometimes they gain even more weight than before they began the diet! Also, diets can be very isolating and restrict us from being social—that's neither fun nor sustainable.

What food philosophy do you recommend?

I truly recommend a food philosophy that "all foods fit." No, that absolutely does not mean eating cupcakes or kale for all meals. When all food is permitted, the balance of foods is easier, as we are not fighting cravings or restricted foods. If you're "allowed" to eat your favorite cookie every day, it's not as exciting as just having it once a month and then bingeing on it. My goal with all my clients is to be able to have fun with food while living a truly healthy, balanced life. Being healthy and balanced and finding joy in your life means that food plays just one role in one's life, it does not dictate it!

CHAPTER 4

Week 1: Visualize Your Winning Game Plan

"You need a vision of where you want to go, what you want to do, who you want to be someday down the road. Simply put: In your mind, you must program your internal viewfinder toward a performance, toward an achievement, toward a scene that you see taking place in your future... That's your vision."

— Bob Bowman, U.S. Men's Swimming Coach, 2016 Olympics

Olympic athletes have been using visualization to reach their goals since the 1960s (Clarey 2014). Now that you are ready for change, visualizing a decisive victory against binge eating will provide you with the mental clarity you need as you embark on this eight-week plan. In this chapter, you will learn to create visualizations of how you will beat binge eating and of your final success. Rather than focusing on self-blame or external circumstances, you'll concentrate on seeing mental images of yourself taking positive actions and accomplishing your goal. That way, you can direct your energy toward developing an inspiring vision of a new normal—a healthy, attuned relationship with food.

We will start by teaching you how to increase purposeful optimism that has proven benefits. Then we will explain the science of how visualizing helps elite athletes and surgeons achieve optimal performance and difficult goals. By the end of this chapter, you'll create your own mental imagery: your winning game plan.

Believe You Can Win

Start believing that success is possible for you. That may seem difficult if you've tried unsuccessfully to stop binge eating. However, building hope is a helpful attitude when making change because people who are optimistic are more likely to stay positive during stressful times, lean on social support, and exert active control; they're also less likely to be depressed (Conversano et al. 2010). Optimists also tend to believe that negative events are inconstant, external, and specific, and that positive events are more stable and frequent.

Grow Your Optimism

We all make mistakes because we are human. Social scientists hypothesize that we may be wired to focus more on negative events than equivalent positive events because paying more attention to negative events benefits survival (Rozin and Rozyman 2001; Wells, Hobfoll, and Lavin 1999). To counterbalance this negative bias and develop optimism, we can actively exert control over our thinking and coping. Even brief interventions, some as short as one session, that target increasing effective coping and control can improve optimism, hope, and well-being (Seligman 2002).

> *"Believe in yourself. Believe that you can do it!!! You are not alone. I know it's hard, but life on the other side is so worth it!"* —Mia

The power of practicing optimism is evident in a study of undergraduates with depression (Miranda et al. 2017). Those who mentally rehearsed positive future event predictions shifted their thoughts about the future away from depressive certainty and toward positive outcomes. Specifically, participants who reviewed likely positive future events were more inclined than the control group to say yes to the chance that they would be *admired by people* and no to the possibility that they would *regret a major life decision*. Reviewing the facts about both positive future everyday experiences and negative uncommon future experiences led to decreases in depression and hopelessness and increases in positive beliefs about their own future.

We encourage you to expand your optimism. Take note of positive events that are likely to occur in your future. Positive predictions can reinforce how good it feels to achieve and grow—and to live without binge eating.

Below, list positive events that you can predict will occur in your own life during the next six months. Identify with a check mark whether each is *very likely* or *somewhat likely* to happen. Two samples are given at the end.

Positive Events in My Future	Very Likely	Somewhat Likely

Example

I will have a satisfying dinner with a friend without binge eating.	✓	
I will learn to play tennis at a beginner level.		✓

Make Peace with Food

Beating binge eating is a marathon, not a sprint. If you're like most people, you've tried hard to gain traction on changing your eating well before you picked up this workbook. Most people with binge eating struggle for years before seeking help. Believe that this time is different. You are learning what works and practicing how to apply it. Even if you slip and binge eat while using these new skills, view that error as specific and temporary. Mistakes are your opportunity to refine your game plan, they are your springboard for permanent success.

Making peace with food is possible! Many others have been on this path. And each started with a first step, which is where you are now. So let's take another step and predict positive successes ahead.

Let's use math to gather more evidence and embolden your optimism.

During a typical week, how many times do you engage in binge eating? _____

During a typical week, how many meals do you eat *without* binge eating? _____

Refer to your estimates above to answer the following questions. Circle your answer.

Has the number of *weekly* binge eating episodes been *less frequent* than your number of regular (not perfect!) eating?

Yes   No

Has your regular (not perfect!) eating been *more frequent* than times of binge eating?

Yes   No

If you answered yes to the questions above, you have evidence that you are more likely to eat regularly than to binge eat. You are already winning most of the time. Use facts to write an optimistic statement, a positive prediction about your future.

_____

_____

_____

_____

Example: *Binge eating has been less frequent than regular eating for me. In the future, I am very likely to be free of binge eating when I eat my planned meals and snacks, practice research-backed strategies, and bounce back quickly from slips.*

If you answered no to the questions above, the skills in this book will give you the tools to confront this problem and develop positive control. You are already winning some of the time. Use facts to write an optimistic statement, a positive prediction about your future.

———————————————————————————————

———————————————————————————————

———————————————————————————————

———————————————————————————————

Example: I have been able to eat without binge eating some times in the past. In the future, I am very likely to be free of binge eating when I eat my planned meals and snacks, practice research-backed strategies, and bounce back quickly from slips.

Optimism will unleash the power of the visualizations you will soon create when you believe that beating binge eating is not only possible but that it is possible for *you.*

"There will be times when you lose. But this battle is winnable." —Samuel

Visualization: Understand It, Create It, Practice It

Our minds like to create, hear, and watch stories. We are going to help you connect with your imagination and transform that visual storytelling part of your mind into a useful tool. *Visualization* is the practice of seeing a success in your mind's eye. Think of it as optimism in your imagination. In your mind's viewfinder, you will learn to see healthy, intentional eating actions that will become your new normal behavior. You can beat binge eating by turning your imagination into a place to mentally practice the steps to your success.

Have you ever tried visualizing reaching a goal? For example, perhaps once when you were sick in bed you imagined you were back to being healthy and feeling happy again. Reflect on your experience.

———————————————————————————————

———————————————————————————————

The Science Behind Visualizing

Visualization or mentally rehearsing is a way of practicing how you *want to act* and the *outcome you want* without actually having to be in the situation. For example, new pilots use visualization to make their skills automatic. They sit in a chair (or in a parked aircraft) and mentally rehearse every step of a flight plan, checklist, and procedure to ensure mastery—they call it *chair flying*.

How would it apply in your life? Let's say your job is stressful and you are vulnerable to binge eating on your way home. Maybe you want to go to a yoga class instead of bingeing after work. So, under low-stakes circumstances—like in the calm of morning—you mentally practice making the healthier choice. Visualization helps you to be prepared to actually follow through on your intention when the situation arises in real life.

Does visualization work? Yes! Targeted mental rehearsal is associated with increases in reaching a variety of types of goals. An analysis of more than sixty studies showed that athletes who combine mental rehearsal with physical practice experience superior performance (Cocks et al. 2014). Elite athletes and their coaches often use mental rehearsal to enhance performance, increase motivation, prepare for problems, and gain mastery.

In a review of nearly thirty studies on using mental skills training to enhance performance and manage psychological stress for surgeons, researchers found evidence that adding a specific type of mental skills training—mental rehearsal—to live practice improved outcomes, increased confidence, and decreased the time it took to learn new procedures (Anton et al. 2017). Given this strong evidence, they suggest that medical schools use visualization to help teach surgical residents. According to lead researcher Anton and colleagues, "Mental rehearsal can help surgeons mentally prepare for a procedure ahead of time, build their confidence and direct their attention on what is required to perform the procedure, identify potential complications and solutions, and help prime their muscles to physically perform, as the same neural pathways are excited through imagery."

Just like these elite athletes and surgeons, you'll begin using mental rehearsal to visualize success.

Visualization and Binge Eating

Does visualization help with urges and eating behaviors? Yes! Adding visualization can improve outcomes. In mental imagery, you rehearse replacing binge eating default-mode behaviors with new behaviors, thoughts, emotional reactions, and skills, even under stressful circumstances (such as when you experience a trigger). Changing your mental imagery can make you less vulnerable to binge eating by reducing negative core beliefs, negative emotions, and urges.

In fact, the images that represent how you think of yourself in your mind's eye bring about stronger emotional responses than your thoughts. Because of this fact, scientists have started using mental imagery to try to change negative core beliefs and the negative emotions that follow to decrease binge eating. In one randomized control study (Dugue et al. 2018), participants who had negative self-beliefs and a memory of a past social rejection created a revised positive mental imagery script. When they recalled the revised positive mental images, they experienced a reduction in negative self-beliefs and negative emotions, a significant increase in positive emotions, and a decrease in the urge to binge eat. In another study, when people with binge eating used mental imagery rescripting, their negative self-beliefs and the urge to binge eat decreased (Cooper, Todd, and Turner 2007).

Related research suggests that mental rehearsal can *increase* healthy eating behaviors (Armatage 2007). In a study focused on improving eating behaviors on a college campus (Knauper et al. 2011), mental rehearsal had a positive impact on fruit consumption. Student participants who ate the least amount of fruit at the start of the experiment made the most significant improvement when they combined a health intention (such as, "When I go into the dining hall for a meal, I will add fruit to my plate") with the practice of targeted mental rehearsal from a first-person perspective over seven days. Visualizing success can also enhance your overall mood (Miranda et al. 2017)—an extra benefit!

Imagine one healthy eating behavior you plan to add, based on your new eating guidelines. Write it down and be as specific as possible.

_____

_____

_____

Example: I will eat a balanced, satisfying breakfast of oatmeal, walnuts, and blueberries every day at my kitchen table this week.

Now, close your eyes. Picture yourself taking that healthy action.

How Does Visualization Help?

Brain studies reveal that mental imagery produces many of the same patterns of brain activation by exciting the same neural pathways as live actions (Anton et al. 2017). Mental rehearsal impacts many cognitive processes in the brain. And many of these processes—such as increased motor control, attention, perception, planning, and memory—you'll need to stop binge eating (Adams 2009).

By visualizing taking positive actions, your brain is getting trained to make healthy decisions. Mentally rehearsing using science-backed strategies to beat binge eating will create new neural pathways. Just like marathon runners might mentally rehearse each minute of a race, you will mentally rehearse how to navigate meals, snacks, urges, and triggers with healthy coping to reach your goal. In addition, visualizing your success can boost your motivation and build your confidence. Visualization is like a dry run of the real thing.

Identify one mental image of your future success. Maybe you picture something like this: You're lying in bed, your alarm goes off, and you realize that you didn't binge the day before even though you were triggered. You feel relieved, strong, and motivated. Write it down and be as specific as possible.

_____

_____

_____

_____

_____

_____

Now, close your eyes. Picture yourself achieving that success and experiencing positive feelings.

Visualization helps you see the possibility of a life without binge eating. Then it brings that imagery into reality. How? Because when you are caught between reason and emotion, the benefits of mental rehearsal—increased motor control, attention, perception, planning, and memory—can help you stick to your goals and gain mastery. Still not convinced? Let's imagine you are experiencing cravings as you leave a holiday gathering. The host offers you a large container of leftovers, and suddenly you are faced with a difficult dilemma. You know rationally that it's not a good idea to take leftovers home, but you're feeling impulsive and the urge to binge is coming on strong. Very strong. So you accept. On the other hand, if you had visualized this scenario beforehand—*when the host offers me leftovers, I will compliment their meal and graciously decline. I will leave empty handed and feel satisfied by the great evening*—you will have mentally rehearsed what to do and say when triggered. There would be very little struggle with what to do because you'll be better equipped to remember your eating plan and stay aligned with it. Your visualization gave you practice, strengthening your ability to be intentional in real-life situations.

Here is a personal example of how one of us (Gia) used visualization. During her six years of graduate school, she consistently visualized success. She immersed herself in academics and clinical experience, but she went beyond that. Gia mentally rehearsed achieving her goal: being handed her diploma and feeling elated. This image helped her stay optimistic and resilient as she navigated the complexities of being a parent, partner, family member, friend, developing professional, and healthy person. Her visualization also kept her closely connected to her motivation on the road to becoming a psychologist. From the moment Gia started graduate studies, she saw herself joyfully crossing the finish line.

Build Your Own Mental Map of Success

There are two types of visualizations for mental rehearsal: *success visualizations* and *process visualizations*. They tap into common and distinct parts of the brain, and both are effective (Filgueiras, Quintas Conde, and Hall 2018).

- **Success visualizations** are instances of visual imagery focused on your successful outcome—the end result—as if it already happened. In your success visualization, you mentally rehearse your desired outcome, or *what you want*.

- **Process visualizations** are instances of visual imagery focused on the details of how you will exert control over your actions and overcome challenges. In your process visualization, you mentally rehearse *where, when, and how* you'll achieve what you want.

Some of us are external visualizers who see images in a mental rehearsal as if we are watching ourselves on a movie screen. Others of us are internal visualizers who view the images as if we have a camera between our eyes looking out into the world. Either works. If you can do both, there is recent evidence that internal visualizing increases accuracy in some sports performance (Callow et al. 2013).

Think of a goal to visualize. Try using external and internal visualizing. Write about which is most comfortable for you.

_____

_____

_____

_____

Using the steps below, describe your mental imagery as if you could see into the future and had reached your goals. Start by creating an image of what success—stopping binge eating and having peace with food—looks and feels like in your mind's eye.

Create Your Success Visualization Script

What outcome do you want? How do you picture your success? How do you want your relationship with food to be? Make it specific. State it as if it were true. Add in the emotion(s) you would feel if you had already achieved it.

_____

_____

_____

_____

_____

_____

_____

_____

Example: *I feel happy and strong. I stopped binge eating. I regularly practice yoga and no longer use food to cope with stress. I eat for nourishment, energy, health, and satisfaction. I reached my goal!*

Now that you know what success looks and feels like, it's time to visualize how you're going to get there. By mentally practicing action-oriented images, you can increase your ability to eat intentionally and to overcome known barriers, such as urges, getting overly hungry or overly full, triggering places, certain people, and hard-to-handle emotions. Your how-to mental rehearsal will increase your optimism and resilience. Picturing yourself taking purposeful steps toward your goal offers the opportunity to mentally practice facing a wide range of difficult circumstances and effective coping strategies. Then you'll have more confidence, knowing exactly how to act in line with your goals when challenges arise in real time (Hatter, Hagger, and Pal 2015).

There are three components to your process visualization: the when, where, and how of the steps you'll take that will lead you to mastery.

Create Your Process Visualization Script

When will you practice your new normal? Make it specific. State it as if it were true.

_____

_____

Example: *After stressful days at work, I will get into my car and notice the urge to stop at my favorite bakery to binge on food. But I will drive right past it. I eat breakfast, lunch, and snacks so my body is well fueled before I leave work. I eat dinner and an evening snack later.*

Where will you eat your meals and snacks? Make it specific. State it as if it were true.

_____

_____

_____

_____

Example: *I will drive right past the bakery to the yoga studio, where I see myself happy to be checking in for class. I eat at home, at work, with friends, colleagues and family. I eat intentionally in environments that support my values and honor my body's hunger and fullness cues.*

How will you follow your plan? Identify potential obstacles and ways to overcome them. It might help to review your results from the Binge Eating Decoder to predict your most common (thinking, emotional, or behavioral) challenges. Make it specific. State your coping strategies as if they were effective. Add in the emotion(s) you would feel if you had already achieved it.

_____

_____

_____

_____

_____

_____

_____

Example: *I actively follow my plan to go to yoga after work, rather than use food to cope. It is a predictable, positive way to manage stress. I feel happy, optimistic, and motivated after yoga. I am stronger when I experience distressing emotions and stress, and I don't let them rule my decision-making. When I notice an urge to stop at the bakery to binge eat, I remind myself that urges and feelings come and go in time, and I don't let them sabotage me. I am thankful for taking this winning step to health.*

Edit Your Visualizations

Before you finalize and begin to practice, review your visualizations. Do your words paint a picture of mastery and inspire you? If not, edit them. Copy your final visualizations on the next page. You can also download the visualization forms from http://www.newharbinger.com/43614.

My Success Visualization

How do you imagine success in your mind's eye?

Describe it as if you have already achieved it. Add in the positive emotions that accompany your success.

_____

_____

_____

_____

_____

_____

_____

_____

_____

_____

_____

_____

_____

_____

_____

My Process Visualization

Use words to paint a mental picture.

When and where will you eat? How will you achieve success and overcome obstacles? Add in the positive emotions that you'll experience as you successfully navigate each step along the way.

_____

_____

_____

_____

_____

_____

_____

_____

_____

_____

_____

_____

_____

Begin a Daily Practice

Every morning, find a quiet space. Take a few relaxing breaths. Slowly read your success and process visualizations silently or aloud. Then repeat your success visualization at night. Don't just read the words. Remember that images are more powerful, so picture each word as an image, experience your senses, and feel the emotions associated with winning as you ingrain your positive behaviors and desired outcome in your mind.

After reading both of your visualizations, journal about what you *feel* as you see those mental pictures of success.

_____

_____

_____

_____

If you won't be near this workbook when it's time to read your success and process visualizations each morning and evening, make a copy of them to take with you.

Update your visualizations as you learn more tools over the next seven weeks. As top athletes do, adapt your process visualization based on each day's schedule, events, or holiday to specify how to achieve success for that day. At the end of each of the following chapters, as you develop your tool kit and practice intentional eating, use whatever works to revise your visualizations.

Q&A with Robert Corb, PhD

Can you share an example of how you use visualization to lead athletes to greater levels of success?

Early in my career as a sport psychologist, a Division I track athlete came to me for help in "performing well in big meets." Chris (not his real name) explained that he was about to run in the conference championship in what could be his final intercollegiate track meet. Chris specialized in an event that was long enough event to involve some serious race strategy (higher-level cognitive functioning) but short enough to require a sprinter's mentality during the latter stages of the race. He had a history of underperforming in pressure situations, and he was willing to try anything to break this pattern.

So I asked Chris if he wanted to experiment with me on a new (to me) technique called visualization, or mental rehearsal. I knew the science behind it because I had lectured about it in the sport psychology class I taught. But taking it out of the pages of a book and putting it into real practice was something new.

I asked him to define his outcome goal, and he said that if he ran a personal best time he could win the conference title and possibly qualify for the NCAA regional meet. He gave me his goal time, and we established a set of checkpoints throughout the race that, if he met, he would know that he was on track to meet his goal. Finally, we were ready for the visualization.

We started writing out a script. I asked him to give me as much detail as he possibly could, focusing on all of the senses and being in touch with what feelings were evoked at different points throughout his race. I suggested that, if possible, he should view the world as if he were inside a camera looking out. I had him look at old videos of himself when he had raced well, to remind himself of what that felt like.

Chris sat quietly and listened as I read through his script. After each trial, we tweaked the script a little bit until Chris was satisfied that it accurately portrayed what he hoped would happen on race day. We recorded the script and he listened to the audio every night until his conference championship two weeks later.

The Monday after his conference championship, I ran into Chris on campus. He had a huge smile on his face. "Dr. Bob, it went exactly the way we visualized it," he said. "I felt like I had already run the race and knew how it was going to end." Coming into the final turn he was in third place, and just like he imagined, he was able to catch the two runners in front of him. He was even more excited to share the news that he had set a personal best and won the conference championship and was headed to the NCAA regional meet.

Can visualization work for anyone?

Since my work with Chris, I have used visualization with many of my clients. I have worked with musicians and public speakers, and with individuals as well as entire teams. I've come to appreciate that visualization can be used in almost any action or performance-based activity.

Any final tips?

I also use this skill in my personal life on a daily basis. Sometimes it is as formal as the work I did with Chris, but sometimes it's as simple as role-playing in my head.

CHAPTER 5

Week 2: The Seven Rules of Goals That Work

"A goal properly set is halfway reached."

—Zig Zigler

Do you have a list of failed New Year's resolutions, broken commitments to yourself about changing your eating or exercise routines, or unkept promises to stop a bad habit? If you're like most people, you've probably had the disappointing and frustrating experience of setting a goal that you didn't meet. It's easy in the face of these experiences to blame ourselves for not trying hard enough or for not being capable. But it's often the case that we failed at our goals because our *goals failed us*. In fact, goals that are set up incorrectly can doom us before we even get started on our plans for change.

Setting a clear and effective goal can be tricky. The good news is that decades of research in social and organizational psychology have uncovered the key principles that make for a good, motivating goal. These principles have been tested in studies of more than 40,000 people working on eighty-eight different goals (Locke and Latham 2006). This chapter will teach you the seven basic principles of how to set goals that will keep you motivated and help you achieve success where you have stumbled before.

To get started, you'll need to identify a goal you'd like to set related to your health—perhaps one concerning the meal plan you created in chapter 3, increasing your exercise, or getting better control of your blood sugar. We're not going to tell you what that goal should be because, as you'll learn below, it's essential that the goal is meaningful to you. One caveat: make sure that your goal is *not* related to weight (see chapter 3 for a detailed explanation). Over the course of this chapter, you'll learn how to refine your goal to make it as powerful as possible. For now, write your goal in whatever words make the most sense to you:

My goal is:_____

_____

We'll also work through an example goal so that you have a chance to see how this process of refinement works in action.

Example goal: *Walk more.*

Rule 1: Goals must be specific and measurable.

The number one reason most goals fail is that they're too vague (Doran 1981). Plans like "eat healthier" don't provide specific enough instructions about what to do, when to do it, or how much of it to do. What does "healthy" mean? Is a cookie healthier than a piece of cake? What if I eat broccoli once when I normally would have eaten potato chips—have I achieved my goal?

You're much more likely to achieve a goal if it's quantifiable—that is, attached to a number—or if it clearly specifies the exact actions you need to take (Locke 1996). For example, you're much more likely to be successful if you set a goal of eating one serving of fruits or vegetables with each meal. You know what to do (eat a fruit or vegetable), when to do it (when you're eating a meal), and how much of it you need to do (one with each meal) in order to achieve the goal.

Another common trap that people fall into when setting goals is to couch the goal in terms of effort—"I'm going to try my best!" Intuitively, focusing on doing the best you can with the skills you have makes a lot of sense. The problem with trying your best, however, is that it can lead you to accomplish *less*. It's nearly impossible to know for sure whether you're giving maximal effort, which makes it more difficult to get appropriate feedback about your performance, which makes it less likely that you'll stay committed to your goal when the going gets tough. Even worse, setting a vague goal about trying your best also means you're less likely to be satisfied with your performance, no matter how well you do.

Now that you know the first rule, let's update our goals. Our example goal of "walking more" was too vague. We need to make it *specific* and *measurable*.

Revised example goal: *Walk at least 10,000 steps every day.*

My revised goal:_____

_____

Rule 2: Goals should be difficult but attainable.

Have you had the experience of setting a goal that was so unattainable that you felt discouraged every time you thought about it? What about setting a goal so small that it didn't even feel worth your time? When it comes to goal setting, it's important to hit the sweet spot of difficulty: a goal that will feel challenging but doable.

The right level of difficulty is important because people are motivated to expend more effort pursuing goals that are difficult than those that are easy, and they're more likely to persist in the face of setbacks in order to achieve more difficult goals (Latham and Locke 2007). Said another way, the harder the goal is, the harder we try. It's also good for your mood to pick a hard goal; you won't get a mood boost unless you see meeting your goal as a real achievement. On the other hand, it's hard to commit to a goal that is not actually attainable, and it's tough to stay motivated during difficult times if success seems impossible.

It's also important that your goal is something that is largely under your own control. If your goal is to walk more steps than your coworkers, you're not really able to control whether you meet that goal—it's going to depend a lot on the behavior of your coworkers. Research shows that goals that are set as a competition against others tend to feel defeating and lead to a decline in performance over time (Strecher et al. 1995). Comparisons to others can make change seem like it's about ability rather than effort, which leads to negative feelings and a desire to give up. In many ways, goals about being the best are as futile as goals about doing your best—neither works.

Now let's revisit our example goal: walk at least 10,000 steps every day. Is that a difficult but achievable goal? That depends—if you're currently walking about 8,000 steps a day and you can think of ways to work in more walking, then that might be reasonable. However, if you estimate that you're only walking about 3,500 steps on most days, and even fewer on weekends, then you're likely setting yourself up for failure. It would be better to choose a goal that will provide a challenge but also be within the limits of your current fitness and lifestyle. On the other hand, picking a goal that is too close to what you're already doing, like walking 3,800 steps, isn't likely to help your overall fitness much, and it's not likely to feel very motivating. Remember: no challenge, no change.

Revised example goal: *Walk at least 5,000 steps at least five times a week.*

My revised goal: _____

_____

Rule 3: Goals should be short term and time limited.

Another design flaw in some goals is that they're so big and so far in the future that it's almost impossible to see success on a regular basis. For example, if you wanted to save enough money in the next ten years to buy a house, which is a large goal a long time in the future, it might be hard to know how much you really need to save in any given month. Setting short-term goals better allows you to track progress toward meeting your goal (Latham and Locke 1991). For example, if your goal is to save 5 percent of your salary this month, you can check in at the end of each week to know whether you're on pace or whether you need to be doing more to cut expenses. Framing the goal around what you can accomplish in one month also tells you when you should check in on your progress and make any needed adjustments. It's important to build in an endpoint for your goal so that you know when to reevaluate.

Having goals that are too distant can also lead to a delay in getting started (Strecher et al. 1995), because it doesn't feel urgent. The other reason distant goals don't work well is because they don't give you a sense of accomplishment. If you want to save money to buy a house, you're going to have to make a lot of difficult sacrifices along the way. If all of those sacrifices seem to add up only to a drop in the bucket for a payoff really far in the future, you might not be so motivated to stick with it. On the other hand, if you can see each month that you're meeting your targets, you're more likely to feel proud and keep going even when it feels difficult.

That said, you may have big ambitions in your life that will take a long time to accomplish, like getting a degree, learning a new skill, or saving enough money for retirement. It's fine and even desirable to have those large accomplishments serve as a source of inspiration; just be sure to also set short-term goals that break down that big objective into smaller pieces. For example, if your goal is to stop binge eating once and for all—a fantastic long-term goal—don't forget to also set short-term goals that will help you along the way, like completing the exercises in one chapter of this book each week.

Revised example goal: *Walk at least 5,000 steps at least five times a week for the next four weeks.*

My revised goal: _____

_____

Rule 4: Goals should be important to you.

It's easy to get pulled into a particular goal because others are doing it, like a coworker who signed up for a 5K run or a celebrity promoting a new diet. However, adopting other people's goals generally doesn't work. You're much more likely to achieve a goal when you feel personally committed to it—that way you are more likely to stick with it when the going gets tough (Locke 1996).

Imagine your boss coming in to tell you that you have to work an extra four hours a week, with no explanation. How motivated would you feel? Contrast that feeling with the way you might feel if you personally chose to work four extra hours a week because you thought that would help you get a promotion. You're more likely to put in the extra time when you see the goal as important and worthwhile for you.

Although it might seem obvious that goals should feel personally meaningful, it's surprisingly easy to get sucked into goals that we feel we "should" follow or that we see other people pursuing. You also need to feel ready to make the kinds of changes that will be required to meet your goal. That's why we're not suggesting a goal for you in this chapter—it's important that you evaluate whether the goal you're setting is really what you want for yourself right now (and not what a doctor, family member, or spouse is pushing you to do).

In addition to figuring out whether the overall goal matters to you, it's important to be clear about why the particular level of success you've set is meaningful (Latham and Locke 2007). For instance, if your goal is to get all top marks on your next performance review, but you know you'll get the same bonus even if you only get satisfactory ratings, it may be hard to put in the extra work. If you get the sense that doing less would be just as good, either adjust your goal to that easier level or dig deeper to figure out what the extra payout would be if you put in some extra sweat equity.

For this step, rather than revise your goal, take some time to write out why this goal is important to you. How is it in line with your values? How will your life be better if you achieve it? Why is the particular level of achievement you set better than doing less?

Example goal: *Walking at least 5,000 steps will improve my strength. If I can achieve that goal most days of the week, I'll build enough fitness to be able to chase my children around the playground more easily, and I'll be more confident saying yes to physically active plans with friends. It will also help my back pain, so I'm less cranky with my partner and children at the end of the day.*

My goal is important to me because: _____

_____

_____

_____

_____

If you determine that your goal isn't a good match for your current life priorities, feel free to revise it here:

My updated goal: _____

_____

_____

_____

_____

Rule 5: Goals should be stated positively and framed for gain.

One of the fundamental principles of goal setting is that it's easier to add a new behavior than it is to subtract a behavior. Goals that tell us what we're supposed to stop doing, without telling us what we're supposed to do instead, are likely to fail. In fact, focusing on what we *don't* want to have happen can make it even more likely that we engage in the behavior we're trying to stop.

For instance, if you want to stop biting your nails, your brain will be checking in about whether you're biting your nails, which will—you guessed it—make you want to bite your nails. Positively stated goals, on the other hand, are useful because they call to mind the action we're aiming toward and make that behavior more likely to happen (Day and Tosey 2011). Therefore, it would be better to set a goal to doodle for five minutes whenever you feel the urge to bite your nails.

Talking to yourself in a positive way about why you want to achieve your goal can also help you stay motivated (Locke 1996). Telling yourself, "If I keep biting my nails, I will look unprofessional and sloppy" will not be as powerful in the long term as moving toward something positive. Using non-food rewards is an excellent way to set up your goals so that you're moving toward something positive. For example, you might agree to get a manicure on any week when you bite your nails two or fewer times. In that scenario, you're working toward something you want, and the sight of your nails is a reminder of what you are moving toward. It won't always be necessary to maintain this reward system. But it's harder to create a habit than it is to maintain it, so a reward can be a great incentive in the beginning of the habit change process.

Similarly, it's important to see setbacks as a chance to learn rather than as a failure (Latham and Locke 2007). Put another way, never making an error is probably a sign that your goal is already in your comfort zone and is not sufficiently challenging. For example, if you miss your walking goal and think to yourself, *Well, there you go, you failure, you'll never be able to do it!*, you will feel discouraged and likely to give up on your goal altogether. However, you will be more motivated to stick with your goal if you look back on that week's setback as an inevitable part of learning to do something new. Try to evaluate the experience to figure out what's different on the weeks when you do meet your goal versus those when you don't. And then, you guessed it, update your goal!

Revised example goal: *Walk at least 5,000 steps at least five times a week for the next four weeks. Reward myself by buying a new song for my playlist each week that I hit my goal.*

My revised goal: _____

_____

_____

_____

Rule 6: Goals should be public.

It's natural to feel nervous about letting other people know about the goals you're setting, especially if you're afraid you might not be successful. But keeping your goals private might limit your ability to achieve them. Letting other people know about your goals increases your commitment and accountability, which increases the likelihood that the goal will be achieved (Hollenbeck, Williams, and Klein 1989). It's much harder to slack off when other people are checking in on your progress. In addition, making goals public allows you to access the kinds of support that might help you in your journey. For example, other people can provide suggestions, advice, or even direct help, like offering to switch your brunch plans to a date to walk around the park. It will also allow others to be more understanding about the changes you're making in your life and to offer you encouragement when things get difficult.

> *"I can't be an island in a solo journey. I was that island for years in active BED. It is not the way to freedom."* —Catalina

Making your goals public does not mean that everyone in your life has to know about every goal you have. You probably have a clear sense of with whom you can share your goals—someone you can count on to be helpful and supportive. However, if you can't think of anyone who would be a good fit for the goal you're setting, consider turning toward an online community. You can find social support groups on social media for almost every kind of goal out there. If you have a Twitter account, you're welcome to tweet us at @Psych_Secrets and we'll be happy to be your cheering squad! Take a minute now to identify a few people or groups with whom you'd like to share your goal.

Example goal: *I will share my goal with my spouse and my boss (so she knows why I'm wearing sneakers in the office). I will also ask my neighbor to meet me for a weekly walk on Fridays and share my goal with my Twitter followers.*

I will share my goal with: _____

_____

_____

Rule 7: Goals should be tracked and reevaluated.

Setting a goal is just the first step to success—it won't get you anywhere unless you take some actions toward that goal and then evaluate how it went (Locke 1996). The best way to keep track of your progress is by writing it down or depicting it graphically. Keeping track "in your head" is likely to lead to confusion, intentional or unintentional fudging of the results, and additional mental strain. A visual representation of results can be particularly rewarding, as you see your progress build over time. Some ideas for how you might track your progress visually would be marking an X, thumbs up, or smiley face on a calendar for each day you accomplish your goal, creating a graph for the number of times per day or week you engage in a particular behavior, or keeping a written log. There are numerous online apps that allow you to track progress in particular goals. Be sure to set aside a regular time to track progress based on the timeline you built into your goal at Rule 3.

Keep in mind that your goals are not set in stone. The objective is to track whether you are meeting your goals and adjust accordingly. If you're having trouble meeting your goal for a few weeks in a row, consider whether you need some additional support or whether starting with a somewhat smaller goal may be more appropriate for now. If you are consistently succeeding in meeting your goal, it might be time to increase the challenge a bit.

Let's say that you don't meet your step count goal for two weeks in a row. You might first check whether there was some unusual reason for that (like having the flu) or whether you might need some additional support (like new sneakers that would make walks more comfortable, or a plan to go walking during your lunch hour). If there isn't a clear answer in either of those categories, you might decide to reset your goal to 4,000 steps and try that for a few weeks. On the other hand, if you're getting your steps in on most weeks, you might add in an extra day so you're aiming for six days a week, or increase your target to 6,000 steps a day.

People are sometimes afraid that they won't be able to cope with the disappointment if they don't meet their goal. However, with the right mindset, that disappointment can be turned into greater effort, or a readjustment to a more appropriate goal, rather than giving up on the goal altogether. Identify the thoughts that have led you to abandon goals in the past. Focus on how to learn from this experience rather than treating it as the end point. Not meeting a goal does not mean you're incapable of meeting that goal—it just means that things went awry this time, and with some careful examination of how to get back on track, you can return to your goal with an even better chance of meeting it.

Think of Olympic ice skaters—they fall all the time as they're learning something new, but they don't take the first five or fifty or five hundred failures as a reason to stop. Instead, they watch videos of themselves, get feedback from their coach, make adjustments, and try again. How can you approach your "failures" with an attitude of learning from it, just like an elite athlete would?

Revised example goal: *Walk at least 5,000 steps at least five times a week for the next four weeks. Check the number of steps on my phone or smartwatch each night before bed, and check my weekly progress on Sunday mornings. Reward myself by buying a new song for my playlist each week that I hit my goal.*

My revised goal:_____

_____

_____

Binge eating may have interfered with your ability to successfully move toward larger, meaningful life goals in the past (Murphy et al. 2012), but you now have all of the information you need to set and start achieving your goals. We'd like you to create one more goal, one that has nothing to do with food or exercise but that would promote happiness or a sense of accomplishment in another domain in your life. As you'll see throughout this book, binge eating is about food and not about food. We want you to be working toward both health goals that prompted you to pick up this book and non-health goals that impact your day-to-day happiness.

My second goal: _____

_____

_____

Take a second now to make sure that your new goal follows all of the seven rules of effective goal setting:

- ☐ Is my goal *specific* and *measurable?*

- ☐ Is my goal *difficult* but *attainable?*

- ☐ Is my goal *short-term* and *time-limited?*

- ☐ Is my goal *important to me?*

- ☐ Is my goal *stated positively* and *framed for gain?*

- ☐ Do I have a plan to make my goal *public?*

- ☐ Do I have a plan to *track* and *reevaluate* my goal?

With these guidelines in place, you're set to have your goals propel you toward success.

CHAPTER 6

Week 3: Change Your Thinking

"Change your thoughts and you will change your world."

—Norman Vincent Peale

Take a moment right now to pause reading and just sit quietly. Try to do nothing for a few minutes. Notice what happens in your mind once you're not reading anymore, and then come back.

Did you find that within a few seconds your mind was creating lots of thoughts? You didn't have to choose to start thinking—the thoughts probably just appeared, maybe returning to something stressful going on in your life, planning for what you need to do later, or even telling you that reading this book is not going to help you. For all of us, our thoughts are a constant companion throughout our days and not always a helpful one. Learning to observe your thoughts, evaluate how true and helpful they are, and build more productive ways of thinking are the next steps in your journey to overcome binge eating.

Negative patterns of thinking can contribute to binge eating because they can cause sadness or anxiety, poor body image, or urges to binge eat. Changing negative patterns of thinking is one of the most powerful components in beating binge eating. In fact, the form of therapy based on changing thoughts, called *cognitive behavioral therapy* (CBT), is one of the most effective forms of treatment for binge eating disorder. Nineteen studies using CBT to treat BED showed that people who received cognitive behavioral treatment were nearly seven times more likely to completely stop binge eating in comparison to people who did not receive this therapy (Vocks et al. 2010).

In this chapter, you will learn how to catch and change thoughts contributing to negative emotions, combat the four types of thoughts most likely to lead to a binge, and effectively manage thoughts about your own body.

The Power of Thoughts

Most of us intuitively believe that our feelings are a direct and inevitable response to the situation we're in. However, CBT teaches us that our emotions and actions are instead determined by the way we think about our situations.

Imagine smiling and waving to your boss in the hallway, only to have her seem to scowl at you and walk by. What thought would pop to your mind?

_____

_____

Let's look at how your thoughts affect your responses to this hypothetical situation. Perhaps your thought is something like, *Oh no, she's mad at me… I bet I made a mistake in that last report… Maybe I'm going to be fired.* Take a moment now to write down the emotions you'd likely feel and the actions you'd likely take if you had that thought:

Emotions: _____

_____

Actions: _____

_____

You'd probably feel some kind of anxiety about the bad things that might happen if your boss is upset. Your behavioral response might be to reread old emails you've sent her or to ask colleagues if they know anything about someone getting fired. That anxiety might also fuel some negative actions meant to dull the anxiety, like overeating, avoiding work you're supposed to do, or even planning a binge for later in the day.

Now let's imagine a different response to the situation with your boss. Let's pretend that after your boss ignored you in the hallway you thought, *Wow, she seems like she's in a bad mood today! I wonder what has her so stressed out. She's been under a lot of pressure recently.* What emotions might you experience and actions might you take in response to that way of thinking?

Emotions: _____

_____

Actions: _____

_____

If your train of thought suggests that she wasn't intentionally ignoring you, you're less likely to feel anxious. In fact, you might even feel some compassion or concern for her. You're unlikely to still be thinking about that interaction hours later. Your behaviors would also be much more adaptive—getting back to the work that needs to be done and sticking to your healthy-behavior plan.

The thoughts that immediately pop to mind after an internal or external experience are called *automatic thoughts* (Beck 2011). They're called *automatic* because they come to mind quickly in response to a situation or an internal experience, without much deliberation or conscious choice. When these thoughts pop up, you probably assume that they're true—people treat their thoughts as a "given" and respond accordingly. However, you can learn to catch and challenge unhelpful thoughts so that they don't lead to binges.

Identifying Your Thoughts

Let's begin by finding a recent time when your thoughts might have sent you heading in an unhelpful direction. Think of the situation you were in right before your last binge episode (or the moment when you started planning it). Put yourself back in that situation as fully as possible: Where were you? Who else was there? What was going on around you right before that emotion or behavior happened? For now, focus just on the facts of the situation not your interpretation of the facts.

The facts of the situations: _____

_____

_____

_____

Example: I was invited to the party of a neighbor I don't know very well. I went but then I realized I didn't know anyone there other than the host, and she was busy with other guests. I started eating as a way to make myself look busy.

Now tune in as much as you can to your thoughts—the way that you were talking to yourself at that moment in time. What was your internal monologue telling you about the situation you described above?

My thoughts in that moment: _____

_____

_____

_____

Example: *I shouldn't have come here. Everyone else here has friends. I'm terrible in these kinds of situations. Everyone can tell that I'm an awkward loser.*

Take a moment to underline the one thought that was most upsetting or that contributed most strongly to your reaction. In the example above, the most upsetting thought was "Everyone can tell that I'm an awkward loser." Often, our thoughts get more distressing as they build on each other, so later thoughts are a good place to look for the most upsetting thought. If you're having a hard time finding it, take each thought in turn and ask yourself, *If I didn't believe this thought, would I have felt and behaved in the same way?* When the answer is no, you've found your key thought!

Challenging Your Thoughts

Once you've identified the thought that's causing problems, it's time to evaluate that thought on three dimensions: is it *accurate, balanced,* and *complete* (Miranda et al. 2006)? The goal is to take a neutral-observer stance in evaluating our thoughts, like a scientist or a judge.

A good way to get started is to ask yourself whether the thought is accurate in its current form. If you were in a court of law, would a judge accept the content of this thought as 100 percent true? Weighing the evidence for and against a thought can help identify ways in which the thought is inaccurate. You can also examine the situation to see if there are any relevant facts that are not included in your thought.

Let's go back and evaluate the evidence for the problematic thought you underlined earlier in the chapter:

Evidence that this thought is true: _____

_____

_____

Example: *Everyone else at the party is talking to each other and I don't have anyone to talk to.*

Evidence that this thought is false: _____

_____

_____

Example: *No one seems to be noticing me much, let alone thinking about how awkward I am. They seem pretty engaged in their own conversations. I can't read other people's minds.*

Any facts left out of this thought: _____

_____

_____

Example: *It's possible that all of these people have met each other before. It would make sense for me to feel a bit awkward given that all of these people are new to me.*

It can be hard to evaluate our own thoughts. Often, our thoughts intuitively "make sense" or "feel true." It takes a conscious, deliberate process to find the flaws in our own thinking. If you're feeling stuck with a challenging thought, here are some strategies that can help (Miranda et al. 2006):

- **Check with another person you trust.** People outside of the situation can sometimes offer a more balanced perspective. A confidant may also have information that helps us to reassess the accuracy of our thought. Example: *Check with a friend about whether they have felt awkward in similar situations, or ask the host whether she think others noticed me.*

- **Get more data.** Design an experiment to collect more information to test out the thought. Example: *Try starting some conversations and see if people at the party would be willing to talk.*

- **Befriend yourself.** Ask yourself what you would say to a friend or loved one who was in your position. What advice or encouragement would you give them? Example: *I would say it's normal to feel awkward when you don't know anyone, but you're awesome and these people would be happy to talk to you.*

- **Check for accuracy.** Check whether you can be 100 percent sure that your initial thought was accurate, and if not, acknowledge that uncertainty. Example: *I can't be sure if other people are noticing me or judging me.*

- **Add what else is true.** Acknowledge what is true in your thought, and then add in a "but…" statement that includes additional information. Example: *I do feel a bit awkward in this situation, but I also have friends who don't think I'm awkward.*

- **Reaffirm your own ability to cope.** When you are triggered, you may automatically want to avoid the feelings. Can you instead remind yourself that you can ride out the feelings, that this moment is temporary? Tell yourself that you can get through it. Example: *Even if this party is a bad experience, I can get through it without overeating. And, in a few days, it won't even matter.*

Once you've gathered all of the facts related to your thought, it's time to build a thought that is more accurate, balanced, and complete. The goal is not to create an overly optimistic thought; the goal is a thought that is a fair reflection of the truth.

Take a moment now to write out your more helpful thought: _____

_____

_____

_____

Example: It's normal to feel a bit anxious in new social situations, and it doesn't mean I'm a loser. I can meet new people here if I try.

Take a moment now to check in about how your reaction to your situation would have been different if you had been able to generate this more helpful, balanced thought. How would your emotions or behaviors been different?

_____

_____

_____

_____

Example: I would have started a conversation instead of overeating. I wouldn't have felt so bad about myself, and I probably wouldn't have had a full-on binge when I got home.

> *"The thinking piece is so key! It's almost like 'fake it till you make it' sometimes. You have to choose what to focus on."* —Hailey

The goal for this week is to build a more helpful thought at least once per day, preferably in the moment that you're feeling upset. Use the worksheet at the end of this chapter to prompt you through the steps of creating a more helpful thought.

Unhelpful Thoughts About Food

Thoughts about food are a key component of the binge eating cycle (Mason and Lewis 2015). Experiences like sadness, anxiety, and stress only lead to binge eating if they cause problematic thoughts about food in response. Catching and targeting unhelpful food-related thoughts is essential in breaking the binge eating cycle. There are four types of thoughts about foods that are strongly associated with binge eating, and this section will teach you how to identify and challenge each type.

Loss of Control Thoughts

The first type of unhelpful thought about food is the belief that you cannot control yourself around a given type of food. These are thoughts such as, *If I eat one bite, I'll eat the whole cake* or *I'm addicted to chips—if I see them anywhere, I eat them.* Thoughts of this kind are associated with binge eating (Glasofer et al. 2013) because they become a self-fulfilling prophecy. These thoughts are also not balanced—you're focusing in on times when you experienced a binge with a certain food, rather than recognizing that you've experienced both *control* and *loss of control.*

Write down any thoughts you tell yourself about being out of control with food:

_____

_____

_____

_____

Using the strategies you learned in this chapter, come up with a more balanced and helpful statement you can say to yourself:

_____

_____

_____

_____

Example: *I have sometimes binged when I was around that food, but there have also been some occasions when I was able to stick to my eating plan.*

If you can't identify times when you have been in control around feared foods, another helpful tactic is to check how much power you're giving to the food itself. Try creating a statement you can use that helps you reclaim a sense of control:

_____

_____

_____

_____

Example: *Ultimately, I am in charge of what I eat; food does not make me do anything.*

All-or-Nothing Thoughts

Another particularly risky thought that often pops up before binges is that if you've broken your diet rules at all, you may as well "go all in" and binge. This kind of all-or-nothing thinking about food triggers binges because even small deviations from ideal eating can be perceived as failure or as a reason to "reset the clock" (Lingswiler and Crowther 1989). Put another way, you decide to binge now and then return to your goal of not bingeing at a later time. If you find yourself falling into this thinking trap, it's likely a sign that you are thinking about foods in an overly rigid way—defining some foods as "bad" and some as "good," or striving for an unrealistic ideal of a healthy diet.

> *"Eating five unplanned extra cookies at lunch doesn't mean I need to give up and binge because I blew it. Five extra cookies doesn't mean I'm a failure and deserve to fail. Five extra cookies doesn't mean I need to eat the whole box... Five extra cookies are just that. Five extra cookies."* —Victoria

Write down any unhelpful beliefs you have about certain foods or needing to follow a particular way of eating:

_____

_____

_____

_____

Overly rigid food rules and avoidance of "bad" foods are a key part of the binge eating cycle, and one of the most important reasons to free yourself from the diet mentality (as discussed in chapter 3). Helpful thoughts acknowledge that no foods are all bad—remember that your food plan needs to be flexible enough to accommodate your situation, hunger, nutritional needs, and preferences. Even if you eat in a way that you didn't plan to, that doesn't mean you need to binge or that all of your progress has been erased.

Take a moment now to come up with a more helpful thought you can use when you're having all-or-nothing thoughts about your food choices:

_____

_____

_____

_____

Example: *Just because I ate four slices of pizza doesn't mean my binge eating prevention plan is out the window. I can get back on track right in this moment without bingeing.*

Obsessive Thoughts

Obsessive thinking about food or planning for the next binge is also a barrier to breaking the binge cycle. Binge eating is often preceded by preoccupation with thoughts about food (Lingswiler and Crowther 1989), and many people find that once they're on the mental train of planning a binge, it's difficult to get off.

One of the best ways to stop obsessive thinking is to engage in an absorbing, somewhat challenging activity that requires your concentration. Some examples of activities that can stop obsessive thoughts are playing a musical instrument, learning a foreign language, working on a puzzle or timed game, playing a sport, doing tai chi, reading an engaging book, or meditating.

List here at least three activities that you can use to refocus your mental energy when you are obsessively planning a binge:

_____

_____

_____

Avoiding Food Thoughts

The last kind of unhelpful thought pattern that contributes to binge eating is trying *not* to think about food at all. Although an obsessive focus on food is not helpful, trying to banish thoughts of food altogether is unlikely to help and may, in fact, make the situation worse. A large body of research has shown that *thought suppression* backfires (Wegner et al. 1987).

Want to see the failure of thought suppression in action? Right now, close your eyes and try really hard not to think about a bright yellow giraffe for two minutes. Set a timer on your watch or phone, and don't do anything in particular other than avoid thinking about giraffes. Come back once you've done the experiment.

Did those pesky giraffes make an appearance in your thoughts? Chances are that they did pop up a few times even though they probably weren't on your mind at all today before reading this chapter. That's because trying to suppress a thought actually creates a preoccupation with the thought you're trying to avoid, a sort of mental radar that's constantly scanning to check if the banished thought has popped up (Wegner 1997).

So what are you supposed to do if you aren't supposed to obsess about food but you also aren't supposed to avoid thinking about food? Instead, try acknowledging the thought by naming it. You might say, *There are those doughnuts again!* and let your mind move on naturally to the next topic in your stream of consciousness.

Unhelpful Thoughts About Your Body

Does your mind harbor negative thoughts about your body? Many people who binge eat have a negative internal commentary on weight, shape, or size. In one study, researchers asked women to stand in front of a mirror for ten minutes while wearing a leotard and say aloud every thought that came to mind (Hilbert and Tuschen-Caffier 2005). Women who had BED were much more likely than women who did not binge eat to express negative thoughts about their bodies, and a follow-up test revealed much greater body dissatisfaction among the women with binge eating. If the thought of standing in front of a mirror for ten minutes in a swimsuit makes you uncomfortable, chances are that you also have unhelpful body image thoughts, whether or not you're aware of them most of the time.

The impact of these negative thoughts are worsened when people place undue importance on weight and shape—that is, they give body shape and size more significance than they need to have (Grilo 2013). Pervasive cultural messages equate thinness (for women) and muscularity (for men) with beauty and health. These messages ignore the inherent diversity of body shapes and sizes, setting up unrealistic and unattainable standards. Striving for these unattainable standards generates deep-seated body dissatisfaction, even self-hatred, that leads to the diet mentality and, for some people, straight into the binge eating cycle.

Letting thoughts about your appearance play a big role in how you feel about yourself as a person contributes to psychological pain. Studies show that putting a lot of emphasis on weight or shape also contributes, ironically, to more binge eating (Grilo et al. 2013). Common thoughts that indicate an overvaluation of weight and shape include *I'm waiting until I've lost weight to start dating* or *I can't be happy unless I look a certain way.*

Another clue that you might be overvaluing this domain of your identity is spending a lot of time thinking about your weight or feeling bad about your body. Some people overvalue weight or shape to the extent that it gets in the way of living their lives—for instance, they might not be willing to go to the beach or play sports because they fear being judged negatively or because they're feeling bad about their appearance.

Take a moment to write down any messages you've internalized from the media or from people in your life who hinder body positivity:

_____

_____

_____

_____

_____

You might be saying to yourself, *But I have to lose weight to be happy!* You might believe that you can't be a good romantic partner, worker, or community member until you reach a certain weight. That is a sentiment we have heard from many clients who have eating disorders. Fortunately, that thought is not accurate.

We have worked with individuals who were happy with themselves and engaged in the world regardless of weight, and we have treated men and women of every weight who felt stymied and depressed by their bodies. It's simply not the case that weight determines happiness, just like it's not true that weight determines health. Can you think of any role models who don't conform to the body shape ideal?

Using the skills you learned earlier in this chapter, try to challenge any thoughts that are coming up around needing to attain a certain weight or appearance before you can engage meaningfully and happily in the other parts of your life:

_____

_____

_____

_____

_____

Example: *Most of the happiest moments in my life had nothing to do with the scale or my appearance. I have aspirations in my life that are bigger and more important than making my body look a certain way.*

> "When I struggle with body image today, I try and switch my thoughts to amazement and gratitude for what my body can do—grow, deliver, and feed a baby!—rather than how it looks. When I go for a hike, I feel strong and grateful that my body can do this. Thinking about how much my body does for me, despite years and years of abuse from me, makes me tear up with gratitude... Learning and practicing self-compassion instead of berating myself helped a lot." —Hailey

An essential ingredient in beating binge eating is shifting to a healthier and more realistic view of the role of weight and shape in your life (Fairburn 2008). Start by listing all of the parts of your identity that are important to how you evaluate yourself. You might include the major roles you have in your life (for example, as a friend, child, parent, spouse, or worker), the activities that make you feel accomplished (as an athlete, musician, artist, or hobbyist), or the ways that you contribute to the world around you that are meaningful to you (as an activist, volunteer, or member of a spiritual community). If you evaluate yourself on your weight or appearance, be sure to include that on your list as well. Take a moment to write out all of the facets of your identity that you use to evaluate yourself, coming up with as many as you can:

_____

_____

_____

_____

_____

_____

_____

_____

_____

Now, taking the ten most important or salient items on your list, determine the relative importance that you have been putting on each of those parts of your identity. Write them out in ascending order, with 1 being the most important factor that influences your feelings of self-worth.

1. _____

2. _____

3. _____

4. _____

5. _____

6. _____

7. _____

8. _____

9. _____

10. _____

Take a look at how you have prioritized these parts of your identity. Does that fit with your deepest sense of who you want to be? If you found that weight, shape, or appearance was high on your list, ask yourself whether you apply those same standards to other people in your life. Have you judged the worth of your friends by their weight? Or evaluated the talent of an artist or merit of a coworker by the number on a scale? If not, why are you applying those distorted standards to yourself?

Think about how a change in perspective might precipitate profound, positive changes in self-worth. Let's take the case of Maria, a client who has come to us for BED. When she started therapy, she was a forty-year-old single woman working as a professor of anthropology. Despite being smart, ambitious, and likeable, she was lonely, frustrated, and stuck in a rut. She had been pressured to lose weight by her family since she was a young girl. Her self-talk, learned from her family, sounded like this: *If I want to be happy and healthy, I have to change my body. Once I do, then I can date, have fun, and be healthy.*

This belief system kept Maria feeling bad about herself despite her accomplishments, as she focused mostly on her string of failed fad diets. She avoided eating with friends and family, and didn't want to buy new clothes or plan for fun trips until she lost weight. She also didn't like being around her family, especially her mother, who made frequent comments about her diet and weight. Feeling hopeless, she came to therapy saying, "I need help because I'm unhealthy, addicted to sugar and carbs, and have no self-discipline. I want to be able to diet successfully so I can have a good life."

We challenged the premise that the primary thing that should determine her happiness is her weight. To accurately evaluate her health, she got a medical checkup, which she had been avoiding, and found no significant concerns. She began to separate from her family's beliefs about her weight and to find other ways to think about health. She no longer used all-or-nothing thinking about what to eat, what it means to be healthy, and which body types are acceptable. Maria started eating for satisfaction, energy, and nourishment. Her energy improved as she gave up on fad diets, and she felt more confident with colleagues and friends. She started going to family outings again, joined a walking group, hiked with her dog, and began accepting more social invitations. Maria participated in a writers' group to get a jump-start on her next book and took on leadership roles in her department. She began to consider the type of person she might want to date and put herself out there to meet potential partners. In short, she reconnected with the truly important aspects of her identity.

When Maria listed what she now draws from to establish her self-worth, she wrote:

1. Creative and accomplished anthropologist.

2. Caring friend.

3. Excellent mom to my dog.

4. Dedicated and loving daughter, even if I don't always agree with my parents.

5. Leader in my church.

6. Loving auntie to my nieces and nephews.

7. Adventurous traveler willing to go to new places.

8. Committed and inspiring teacher.

9. Supportive mentor to my graduate students.

10. Dedicated to my own health and well-being.

With this broader perspective on identity in mind, reorder your own list to reflect a healthier, happier way of evaluating yourself. Think about all the different parts of yourself that you want to draw from in building your sense of self-worth.

1. _____

2. _____

3. _____

4. _____

5. _____

6. _____

7. _____

8. _____

9. _____

10. _____

What can you do to increase the importance you place on the parts of your identity that are separate from appearance? For example, you might need to start or reengage with activities that are related to other meaningful parts of who you are in the world. If you've stopped doing an activity you used to love, lost connection with your faith or a group of supportive friends, or let responsibilities slide at work or school, incorporate those activities back into your day-to-day schedule. Even a small action, like writing a note to a friend saying that you're thinking about them, can help reconnect you to that part of your identity and increase your life satisfaction. If you spent less time and mental energy focused on eating, food, and appearance, how could you use that energy to reaffirm the other important parts of your identity?

Take a moment here to reflect on at least three ways you can increase your connection with the parts of your identity that are not related to appearance. Make a plan for how you can take concrete action in the next few days:

Healthy identity role	Way to reconnect	Action plan

Example:

Aunt	Let my niece know how special she is to me	Write her a card telling her how proud I am of her

You now have all of the tools you need to identify and challenge unhelpful thoughts. You are aware of the high-risk thoughts about foods that lead to binges, and you have a plan for how to combat them. You also have a more balanced perspective on your identity and a plan for connecting with the parts of yourself that are separate from weight and food.

Use the Helpful Thoughts Worksheet below (or download it from http://www.newharbinger. com/43614) at least once every day this week in response to emotionally upsetting situations or urges to binge. Doing so will help solidify the steps you learned in this chapter. The goal of this deliberate practice is to have this skill become automatic in challenging moments.

If it's too difficult to learn this skill while you're feeling emotional, set aside a time at the end of the day to reflect back on periods of high emotionality or out-of-control behavior. See if you can find a thought that would have helped you get back on track. The eventual goal is to be able to use this skill in the high-intensity moments when you need it most. Remember that catching and correcting unhelpful thoughts can help steer you toward better moods, better food choices, and a better relationship with your body.

Helpful Thoughts Worksheet

The facts of the situation were: _____

_____

_____

_____

My thoughts in that moment were: _____

_____

_____

_____

Evidence that these thoughts are true:_____

_____

_____

_____

Any facts left out of these thoughts: _____

_____

_____

_____

A more helpful thought would be: _____

_____

_____

_____

CHAPTER 7

Week 4: Ride the Waves of Emotions and Cravings

"I am not afraid of storms,
for I am learning how to sail my ship."

—Louisa May Alcott, *Little Women*

Emotions offer us key information about who we are and what we want. They help us to communicate our needs with others. Emotions are with us constantly. They make us *feel* human. When we accept them and move in harmony with them, they can help us to heal, harness motivation, and recognize our need for more closeness or more distance. Emotions are our built-in life-navigation system. They signal us to take adaptive actions and help us to function in the world.

At times—when our emotions are negative, intense, and difficult to handle—we may be tempted to disregard their value and resist them by reaching for quick fixes, such as by using alcohol and other drugs, binge eating, or compulsively working, to name a few. While such habits of emotional avoidance may offer temporary relief, they don't work for long and often make matters worse!

"Becoming aware of and feeling my emotions played a big part in discovering how I was using food. There was a time when I couldn't identify most emotions... The only feeling I was aware of was anxiety. Becoming aware of the emotions I felt helped me to identify triggers and sensitivities. Even before I could stop myself from bingeing, there was value in being able to identify the emotions I felt before the binge... Being able to recognize them and allow myself to experience them without judgment has changed the way I react to my emotions." —Samuel

Take a few minutes to check in with your current emotional awareness. Think about the past twenty-four hours. What specific emotions have you experienced? List all you can recall.

_____

_____

_____

_____

_____

Which emotions are you experiencing right now?

_____

_____

During the past week, how would you describe the average intensity of your emotions on a scale from 1 to 5?

☐ 1   **Peaceful**, as if I'm a smooth stone skipping across the calm waters of a lake.

☐ 2, 3, 4 **Relatively neutral**, as if I'm a skier gliding down the slopes with some effort.

☐ 5   **Intense**, as if I'm white-knuckling it on a thrill-seeker's roller coaster.

Despite the ubiquitous nature of emotions, few of us are taught why we have them or how to manage them. In the absence of better strategies, you may have a feeling, then react automatically or impulsively. If so, you may feel powerless over feelings and your reactions to them—almost like an emotional ball being tossed around in the pinball machine of life. While we can't always control our emotions, we can usually control our responses to them. Your emotional empowerment exists in the space between your feelings and actions. In that space, you have choices.

Coping well with emotions is central to every aspect of life. Effective emotion management brings about an increased potential for self-confidence, healthy relationships, and achievement. Increasing your emotional competence is especially important as you build routines to stop out-of-control eating (Kenny et al. 2017; Leehr et al. 2015; Spoor et al. 2007). The research suggests that binge and emotional eating may be related to difficulty with the following:

- Understanding and accepting negative emotions

- Maintaining goal-directed behavior during intense emotions

- Inhibiting impulsive behaviors

- Using effective strategies to deal with strong emotions

- Tolerating the awareness of not meeting one's own high standards or perceived expectations of others

- Facing problems

If you notice a reciprocal relationship between eating and emotions, the good news is that you can change with emotion management skills. Just as your emotions may be impacting your eating, your eating may be affecting how you feel. You can break this cycle.

How does binge eating impact your emotions?

_____

_____

How do you anticipate your emotions will change when you stop binge eating?

_____

_____

Keep in mind that getting plenty of sleep matters when it comes to handling emotions. Being sleep deprived can significantly impact your emotional functioning by amplifying emotional reactivity (Walker 2017). Without enough sleep, you're more likely to swing from one emotional extreme to the other and to be more vulnerable to binge eating due to a heightened desire for immediate pleasure and reward seeking. If you're not getting an adequate amount of sleep, return to Week 2 to establish a sleep goal that will work.

Now, let's build the skills that will enable you to shift away from emotional avoidance, escape, and impulsivity toward tolerance and chosen responses. Naming emotions and experiencing them can diffuse their intensity and give you more power over them.

Label It

A large body of evidence suggests that a simple, easy-to-use technique—naming your emotions—can be powerful for helping us manage strong negative emotions. It sounds somewhat counterintuitive—why would saying "I feel sad" or "I feel anxious" help us to feel better? You're not the only one wondering. When asked how much naming a negative emotion would help them to feel better, most people thought it would not be a useful strategy (Lieberman et al. 2011). And yet, the science is clear: naming your feelings diffuses their intensity.

Let's look at one example of how it works. Studies that looked at naming emotions in scary situations have found that it can reduce fear. One study exposed people with a spider phobia to a live tarantula, asking them to get progressively closer over time and even to touch the spider (Kircanski, Lieberman, and Craske 2012). Participants were told to name their feelings about being near the spider, try to change their feelings, or try to mentally distract themselves. People who named their fears were less physically anxious the next time they were put near a spider and were willing to get closer to the spider than the people who tried to distract themselves from how afraid they were. All it took was saying the name of the feeling they were having out loud as they were experiencing it. In fact, the people who used the most words associated with anxiety and fear when labeling their emotions got the most benefit—they were the least afraid of the spider in the future. Other research done with brain-imaging technology has shown that naming emotions reduced brain activation in the amygdala, a part of the brain associated with fear and other emotions (Lieberman et al. 2007).

"Learning to cope with emotions played a gigantic role in recovery. I learned to have my emotions closer to the time I was feeling them, especially by staying in my body and learning my body's cues." —Charlotte

Recent studies further clarify the mechanisms related to the role of emotion differentiation in eating behaviors (Jones and Herr 2018). Undergraduate participants who experienced a negative mood but were *not able to label* it ate more than those who experienced a negative mood but were *able to identify* it (Dingemans, Danner, and Parks 2017). Being able or unable to identify particular positive emotions did not seem to have an impact. The authors concluded that identifying and labeling which negative emotions you are experiencing may reduce the connection between emotional distress and emotional eating.

Clues to Emotional Clarity

Start noticing your feelings throughout the day. Sometimes what you feel will be easy to name. Other times, emotions may be confusing and hard to describe. Try using psychology researcher

David Barlow's three-component model when you're unsure how to describe your emotional experiences: check in with your thoughts, body, and behaviors for clues (Barlow et al. 2011).

Emotions may show up in your thoughts. What are you *thinking* right now? What feelings do you notice?

_____

_____

Example: I'm thinking, "I shouldn't have texted my friend to hang out this weekend." I notice that I feel embarrassed and vulnerable.

Emotions may show up in your body. What *sensations* do you notice in your body right now? What feelings do you notice?

_____

_____

Example: I feel sensations in my body—my stomach feels off, like it has butterflies in it, as I prepare for my audition. I notice that I feel excited and nervous.

Emotions may show up in your behaviors. What *behaviors* are you engaging in right now? What feelings do you notice?

_____

_____

Example: I am taking an action—I am walking into the kitchen to grab a bag of chips. I notice that I feel neither hungry nor full. I feel lonely.

Lean In

Naming your feelings is a great start to emotional well-being, but it isn't enough. For example, we have a client who successfully labels the feeling of sadness but consistently reacts by losing control with food. Rather than trying to accept and understand the uncomfortable emotion, he uses a negative habit to escape it. We call that an emotional cycle of *leaning out.*

Alternatively, when you *lean in* to your emotions, you accept all of them—even those that are uncomfortable or distressing. It doesn't mean you passively dwell on negative emotions or allow yourself to fall into a dark hole. Leaning in is active because it enables you to connect the dots between various situations and how you feel. Understanding that link is crucial to improving your effective coping and the actions that follow. Leaning in is also empowering because you'll gain confidence from knowing that there is no emotion you can't handle. Together, labeling and leaning in make you less vulnerable to reactive behaviors (such as turning to food to cope) and more apt to have greater health, better relationships, and more happiness.

Emotions Are Messengers

The purpose of emotions is to help us navigate the world. Even though we may prefer certain emotions over others, emotions are not inherently good or bad. If you are in the habit of denying, escaping, or avoiding emotions, you're missing out on the signals they offer and interfering in a natural human process meant to guide you. Emotions have two important purposes:

1.   To communicate with ourselves and others

2.   To motivate ourselves

Although you can suppress emotions, you cannot rid yourself of them.

Even if you haven't given it much thought before now, you were born to notice and respond to emotions. At the same time, most of us hold on to a bias about emotions. Do you believe it is better to feel happy rather than frustrated? Have you been told "don't be sad"? Consider the danger of having positive emotions only. If babies only showed positive emotions—in an attempt to seem cheerful—they wouldn't cry to be fed, and that unending cheerfulness would be life threatening.

It is risky to deny negative feelings—and not only because doing so is associated with an increase in emotional eating (Dingemans et al. 2017). Let's consider the purpose of some emotions associated with binge eating:

- *Anxiety* is a signal that there may be danger on the way, highlighting our need for safety, focusing our attention on potential threats, and motivating us to take appropriate actions.

- *Sadness* is a signal that we may be experiencing a loss, encouraging us to heal or grieve until we feel strong enough to cope.

- *Anger* is a signal that someone or something may be threatening us, or that there is a disconnection, motivating us to protect or defend ourselves from someone or a situation causing us harm.

- *Guilt* is a signal that we have done something incongruent with our values, propelling us to notice the error and correct our course of action.

All of these very important emotions serve a purpose, including warning us of a grave issue at hand. When we deny or avoid these feelings, we miss an opportunity to acknowledge the issue and then take steps to correct it.

"When I was no longer bingeing or restricting, I thought it would make me happy. But it didn't. It made me incredibly emotional. I was sad all the time. Really sad. But I decided to live in it. I let myself be sad—maybe for the first time in my life. It was horrible and hard. Then, all of a sudden, the sadness went away. And the eating disorder didn't come back! I truly didn't think I was hiding my feelings by having this ED, but I must have been, because once I let myself have that terrible, terrible month of sadness, it all went away. I haven't binged or restricted ever since. That was years ago." —Mia

Now it's your turn to practice accepting that emotions are signals. Answer the following to connect imagined experiences, emotions, and purpose.

If you notice an older person with acute chest pain, what might you feel?

_____

Are these feelings helpful? _____

What's their purpose?

_____

If you hear beautiful music during a concert, what might you feel?

_____

Are these feelings helpful? _____

What's their purpose?

_____

If you earn a high grade in a difficult class, what might you feel?

_____

Are these feelings helpful? _____

What's their purpose?

_____

As you can see from the questions above, our feelings have meaningful, sometimes life-saving messages that guide us.

If you binge eat when your exciting Friday night plans fall through, what might you feel?

_____

Are these feelings helpful? _____

What's their purpose?

_____

It Is Impossible Not to Feel Emotions

Let's think about how attempts at suppressing emotions evolve. Imagine you feel extremely overwhelmed by an upcoming presentation for your job. Without consciously choosing how to manage your strong emotions about this task, you react by avoiding thinking about the project. When you are reminded of the project and feel anxious, you escape the discomfort by spending time with friends, binge eating, or watching TV. These distractions help you feel better *temporarily*. That's because suppressed emotions have a way of popping up again when you least expect it.

"Little by little I got more used to riding the waves of emotions without cutting them off by using food." —Hailey

For example, you might be at a comedy show with a friend a few days before your unfinished presentation is due. While other people are laughing, you have an anxiety attack. You begin sweating and your heart is racing. You're scared, thinking something bad is about to happen. This intense anxiety seems to come out of nowhere. Can you guess what may have triggered the anxiety? Most likely, your emotional avoidance stopped working. Intense anxiety surfaced to get your attention because you had been ignoring the subtle emotions related to your upcoming project. The anxiety is letting you know that there is trouble ahead due to your lack of initiation. Although it feels bad to experience intense negative emotions, they have a purpose. In this situation, your heightened anxious feelings are trying to communicate that there is a problem and motivate you to take actions that will help you cope with the future—by successfully preparing for your presentation.

Just like emotional avoidance didn't help in this example, binge eating doesn't help us to regulate or manage negative emotions—though it may be an attempt to do so.

How Does Leaning In Help Stop Binge Eating?

The strong link between negative emotions and eating offers you powerful *choice points,* a point in time when you can pause before you take any action. Such choice points can happen in just a few minutes or over several hours. By noticing and accepting intense negative emotions, you can create choice points when you consider your options and their consequences, and make a goal-driven decision—one that leads you toward making peace with food. Your willingness to take advantage of emotional choice points, instead of leaning out by defaulting to mindless reactions, gives you a powerful opportunity to exert positive control over your life, along with another tool to stop binge eating.

The research shows that positive moods tend to be higher on non-binge days and negative moods higher on binge days (Dingemans et al. 2017). Specifically, we know that sadness, anger, frustration, disappointment, hurt, loneliness, tension (brought on by the stress of daily hassles), and anxiety are the most common emotional triggers in binge eating (Dingemans et al. 2017). Some people report engaging in binge eating in response to positive feelings, but with less frequency.

If you are more likely to lean out when faced with negative emotions, you may be missing out on potentially powerful choice points. Therefore, let's build your capacity to lean in to negative emotions, a skill that will leave you poised to make choices with long-term benefits.

"Slow down and be patient... Listen to your body and don't allow yourself to rifle past that point you know isn't comfortable. Listen to consequence, action/reaction, use fear to your advantage... Don't trick yourself into justifying your behavior. There is no justifying self-sabotage—and you're worth everything. You're all you got!" —Oliver

Let's now practice leaning in. Use logic to think through the potential lasting benefits of facing your emotions rather than binge eating in response. Complete the following chart.

The last time I felt...	When I experience this negative emotion, I can choose to *lean out*, attempt to avoid it, and binge eat. What are the immediate effects and long-term benefits?	When I experience this negative emotion, I can choose to *lean in* and tolerate it, instead of binge eating. What are the immediate effects and long-term benefits?
...*sad* was when:	Immediate effects: Long-term benefits:	Immediate effects: Long-term benefits:
...*angry* was when:	Immediate effects: Long-term benefits:	Immediate effects: Long-term benefits:
...*frustrated* was when:	Immediate effects: Long-term benefits:	Immediate effects: Long-term benefits:

The last time I felt...	When I experience this negative emotion, I can choose to *lean out*, attempt to avoid it, and binge eat. What are the immediate effects and long-term benefits?	When I experience this negative emotion, I can choose to *lean in* and tolerate it, instead of binge eating. What are the immediate effects and long-term benefits?
... *disappointed* was when:	Immediate effects: Long-term benefits:	Immediate effects: Long-term benefits:
... *lonely* was when:	Immediate effects: Long-term benefits:	Immediate effects: Long-term benefits:
... *hurt* (emotionally) in a relationship was when:	Immediate effects: Long-term benefits:	Immediate effects: Long-term benefits:
... *tense* due to stress was when:	Immediate effects: Long-term benefits:	Immediate effects: Long-term benefits:
... anxious was when:	Immediate effects: Long-term benefits:	Immediate effects: Long-term benefits:

Hopefully acknowledging the *lack of long-term benefits of leaning out* and the *many benefits of leaning in* to even negative emotions strengthens your resolve to implement better emotional strategies and ride out urges!

Identify Your Most Frequent Emotional Triggers

Now you have a clear grasp on the concepts that emotions are messengers and that suppressing certain types of feelings can lead to binge eating or other negative behaviors. It's time to figure out which feelings are most troublesome for you.

Let's practice identifying your emotional triggers. Do you binge eat in response to some or all of the following emotions? Think back over the past six months. Which emotions are present *before* you experience a loss of control with food? Complete the following inventory.

Sadness	Yes	No	Embarrassment	Yes	No
Anger	Yes	No	Regret	Yes	No
Frustration	Yes	No	Boredom	Yes	No
Disappointment	Yes	No	Trouble calming down	Yes	No
Loneliness	Yes	No	Joy	Yes	No
Hurt	Yes	No	Overwhelm	Yes	No
Tension/stress	Yes	No	Guilt	Yes	No
Anxiety	Yes	No	Other: _____	Yes	No
Intense cravings	Yes	No	Other: _____	Yes	No

Reflect on the inventory above. Identify the four emotions that are *most frequently present prior* to episodes of binge eating you have experienced.

1. _____

2. _____

3. _____

4. _____

Journal about what might be different if you began to lean in to these four emotions:

_____

_____

_____

_____

_____

_____

_____

_____

_____

_____

Skills to Respond Effectively

In the remainder of this chapter, you'll gain confidence when you see that you have the ability to handle strong emotions and cope well. Return to these exercises anytime you experience intense emotions or cravings that might otherwise lead to binge eating.

Write Expressively

Writing down your thoughts and feelings about difficult, scary, or traumatic events has been linked to a wide range of positive outcomes, including improved physical health, decreases in negative emotions like anger and depression, improved social relationships, and better school outcomes (Frattaroli 2006). When you experience an upsetting event, write about it three times for at least fifteen minutes each time. Include the facts of the situation and all of your emotions associated with it. Use this tool often to get out of the habit of emotional avoidance. Effectively facing difficult situations and feelings will reduce your risk of binge eating.

Now let's practice acquainting yourself with your ability to handle difficult emotions using *expressive writing*. Identify a situation that is currently causing you some distress. Take fifteen minutes to write down the facts of the situation. Name all of the emotions you are experiencing. Repeat this exercise until you've written on three consecutive days.

Day 1

_____

_____

_____

_____

_____

_____

_____

_____

Day 2

_____

_____

_____

_____

_____

_____

_____

_____

Day 3

_____

_____

_____

_____

_____

_____

_____

_____

What do you notice after writing about this difficulty for the past three days?

_____

_____

_____

_____

Rely on Facts for Motivation

If you binge eat to manage emotions, you may do so hoping that it will make you feel better. The truth is that binge eating will—almost certainly—make you feel worse. Consider a study of 239 female twins who were followed for forty-five consecutive days (Haedt-Matt et al. 2014). Each day after 5 p.m., participants completed questionnaires assessing their daily level of negative and positive emotions, their urge to eat in reaction to those emotions, and associated binge eating behaviors.

Think back to your *most recent* binge eating episode. What *feelings* were you experiencing before?

_____

_____

_____

_____

_____

For study participants, binge eating led to only momentary relief and then, on the following days, participants experienced an increase in negative emotions and no improvement in positive emotions.

After your most recent time of binge eating, what *feelings* did you experience the next day?

_____

_____

_____

_____

_____

Now that you have the facts, you can counter any false beliefs you may have held and focus on tolerating negative emotions instead.

What are the facts about how binge eating impacts your mood?

_____

_____

_____

_____

_____

Reach Out to People (Not Food)

Remember when we mentioned that emotions help you communicate with yourself and others? When you experience intense negative emotions, it is often helpful to share them with supportive people in your life (Corstophine 2006). After all, you are not alone.

"There is absolutely no way that I could have done this alone. No way. I opened up to people." —Isaiah

Let's practice reaching out: with which people in your life could you express your negative emotions? Consider those who seem to accept that negative emotions are a normal part of life.

_____

_____

_____

_____

_____

Describe a situation when reaching out would have been helpful in the past.

_____

_____

_____

_____

_____

Describe a situation when you will reach out in the future.

_____

_____

_____

_____

_____

Everyone experiences negative feelings and difficult situations. Rather than hiding your burdens or reaching out to food, reach out to people to get your needs met. They can provide support, feedback, distraction, soothing, or problem solving.

Promote Positive Emotions

We can experience more than one emotion at any given time. However, when you feel distressed, you may collapse your attention and ruminate on negative emotions exclusively. But you can cope more effectively by resisting this tendency and opting to widen your perspective. *Remember that in the space between feelings and actions, you have choices.* Positive coping thoughts can promote positive emotions that soothe you, give you strength and patience, and balance your emotions in times of upset (McKay, Wood, and Brantley 2007). The goal is not to deny negative emotions or cravings but to simultaneously expand your attention. When you can cultivate positive feelings, you can steady your emotional state and increase your capacity to ride out urges.

The idea is to develop personal statements that cultivate positive feelings. These statements should be grounded in personal strengths or universal truths. When they are authentic, it will be easier to take a step back and respond deliberately rather than react with harmful default behaviors based on temporary emotions. Consider using song lyrics, favorite mantras, inspiring quotes, words of a prayer, or wisdom from a loved one.

> *"When my thoughts stray down a rabbit hole telling me that nutrition isn't worth it, I have to redirect thoughts to prevent self-sabotage. I replace that thought with healthy, hardy thoughts, embracing strength. I tell myself, 'I am strong and want to get stronger.' I embrace my masculine attributes and thrive. How dare some phantom thought process try to prevent me from embracing a normal, thriving self-confidence! Free at last!"* —Oliver

Now let's practice promoting positive emotions.

My Positive Coping Statements

Write ten statements that intentionally cultivate positive emotions in you. After you write each, take a breath, then connect with its meaning.

1. _____

2. _____

3. _____

4. _____

5. _____

6. _____

7. _____

8. _____

9. _____

10. _____

Example:

1. This feels bad, but it's temporary.

2. Like waves in the ocean, feelings come and go.

3. Everyone makes mistakes sometimes.

4. I feel strong when I get through hard times.

5. I have had this feeling before and have been okay.

Place this list where you can easily access it. You can even take a photo of it and save it to your phone. Review these statements daily. The goal is to eventually make these statements come to you automatically when a negative emotion or situation arises. Then you are able to invite positive emotions alongside negative ones.

Empower Your Healthy Self

The goal of empowering your healthy self is to develop the confidence that you are able to face and handle life's challenges. Even if you have used food to cope for many years, you also have a healthy self (Costin and Grabb 2011). When you're experiencing a craving, fantasizing about a binge, or feeling intense negative emotions, ask yourself the following questions:

What would I tell my best friend to do?

How would I treat them in this situation?

The care you feel for your friend can give you a window into healthy, effective coping.

Now let's practice empowering your healthy self: think of a time when you turned to binge eating for emotional coping in the past. Now imagine that your best friend experienced the same situation tomorrow. Write out compassionate, practical advice that you would offer to your friend.

_____

_____

_____

_____

_____

_____

_____

_____

_____

Find Comfort

The sort of comforts that boost your resolve to ride out emotionally difficult times will be unique to you. Take a peek into a few of the nearly limitless paths of comfort that can connect you to your soul, bring about calm, and soothe you.

NATURE

Emerging science suggests that spending time in nature may promote well-being because of its physical and mental health benefits. It is also associated with reduced levels of anger, sadness, depression, anxiety, and physiological responses to stress (Chun, Chang, and S.-J. Lee 2017; Bowler et al. 2010; Kobayashi et al. 2018). Consider the 2018 study by Kobayashi and colleagues who looked at the benefits of *shinrin-yoku,* or forest bathing, which is the practice of taking in the forest atmosphere with the senses. Male university students were tracked while they walked in fifty-seven different forests as compared to fifty-seven different urban areas in Japan. Measurements were taken of the 520 participants' autonomic nervous systems. During walks in the forest, activity decreased in their sympathetic nervous systems (which prepares our bodies to respond to stress) and activity increased in their parasympathetic nervous systems (which controls our bodies in more relaxed and ordinary circumstances). For 62 percent of the participants, forest bathing had a physiological, relaxing impact.

> *"I learned to rewire my brain by finding tangible things to do, like read books, journal, write a gratitude list, take a walk, get in nature, and really, really be in the moment. I also remind myself of the big picture."* —Isaiah

Reflect on your own experiences in nature.

_____

_____

_____

_____

_____

SPIRITUAL PRACTICES

Consider whether you experience comfort in spiritual rituals, gatherings, or activities such as praying, singing, meditating, candle lighting, studying texts, or attending services.

Reflect on your own experiences with spirituality.

_____

_____

_____

_____

ALTRUISTIC FELLOWSHIP

Reflect on times when you may have found comfort in sharing common values and altruistic or compassion-based experiences with a group of people. To help you think about this concept more practically, here are a few examples of potentially helpful fellowship: sharing negative emotions with others in a safe setting, such as a grieving circle; volunteering a service, such as tutoring; or attending mutual-help meetings, such as Alcoholics Anonymous (Kelly and Yeterian 2012).

Reflect on your own experiences with fellowship gatherings.

_____

_____

_____

_____

PLEASURABLE ACTIVITIES

What do you enjoy doing? Is there something you haven't done in a while but that you'd like to do again? Something you've always wanted to try? Do not underestimate even the littlest of things that bring ease into your life. It could be getting a massage, going to the movies, playing an instrument or sport, participating in a book club, drawing, inviting friends over, or using a meditation app.

"One key to recovery has been singing regularly with a thirty-voice women's a cappella group. It keeps my heart-soul flying free and joyously!" —Catalina

Describe an activity that brings you comfort. Don't limit your ideas to the examples we highlighted above.

_____

_____

_____

_____

_____

Make a specific plan. Write about how, when, and where you will engage in this activity, and how it might help you cope with negative emotions.

How, when, and where I will do this activity:

_____

_____

_____

How it will help me cope with negative emotions:

_____

_____

_____

Engage in Positive Actions or Distractions

Strong negative emotions may have led you to out-of-control or impulsive actions in the past. The good news is that changing what you do, just like changing what you think, can positively impact your ability to effectively regulate your emotions. Complete the charts below to identify positive actions and the rewards they may prompt.

List five activities you find enjoyable. Then predict the potential benefits.

Enjoyable activities	Rewards they might lead to
1.	
2.	
3.	
4.	
5.	

Example:

Playing golf	Improving my game and getting outside.
Seeing a movie	Enjoying a story and getting out of my head.
Painting	Being present and creating art.
Taking my dog to the dog park	Doing something nice for my dog and enjoying the movement and time in nature.

Distraction is another effective strategy for regulating your emotions. There may be times when you are not ready to enjoy an activity or confront a problem you are facing. But you know that sitting in your negative emotions and ruminating is not helping. While it may not solve the problem, distraction can offer temporary relief. Depending on how you decide to distract yourself, your actions and thoughts may even lead to positive rewards.

List five positively distracting actions. Then predict the positive benefits.

Positive distracting activities	Rewards they might lead to
1.	
2.	
3.	
4.	
5.	

Example:

Doing laundry	Getting it off my to-do list and having clean clothes for the week ahead.
Taking my car to the car wash	Having a clean car and feeling organized.
Writing out a birthday card for a close friend	Letting her know I care about her.

Review the above lists and their rewards.

Choose one enjoyable activity and journal about what might have gone differently if you tried this rather than turning to food:

_____

_____

_____

_____

Choose one distracting activity and journal about what might have gone differently if you tried this rather than turning to food:

_____

_____

_____

_____

Try Opposite Action

Think back to when you have acted on strong negative emotions, cravings, or impulses. At least sometimes, the outcomes were probably negative. Automatically acting on our negative emotions can make your situation worse! This skill—called *opposite action*—offers you a strategy to regulate intense negative emotions by resisting your temptation to do what you usually do and bring about a better outcome (Linehan 1993). Not only can opposite action help you manage negative emotions, it can lead to new emotions (McKay et al. 2007).

"After twenty years of bingeing, I had destroyed my body. I knew I had to finally get bingeing out of my life. I learned tools to manage the feelings I was numbing... I had to do the things that scared me and caused discomfort. It was terrifying. A huge thing that helped was that I started to do the opposite. When something scared me I just did it anyway."
—Isaiah

Tips for taking opposite action:

- Name and accept what you are feeling.

- Identify the automatic behavior that the negative emotion or craving is leading you toward.

- If that impulse is not in your best interest, identify an opposite action that is better for you.

- Act opposite to create better outcomes.

Ready to practice taking opposite actions? Complete the chart below to see how you can use opposite actions to keep negative emotions and cravings from leading to negative behaviors. Apply this skill to stop binge eating.

When I experience this emotion...	Sometimes I have reacted automatically and made matters worse, such as:	In the future, I can try this opposite action:
Sadness		
Anger		
Frustration		
Disappointment		
Loneliness		
Hurt		

Tension or stress		
Anxiety		

Example:

Sadness	Stay in bed, isolate myself, neglect my responsibilities, curl up, keep my head low, binge eat in secret, feel guilt and shame	Shower, make my bed, stand up straight, reach out to someone, take a step toward one goal, raise my gaze, plan out and eat balanced meals, leave my apartment to take a thirty-minute walk, feel strong and motivated and resilient, offer a genuine compliment to someone

Journal about how taking these opposite actions might have a positive impact on your relationship with food—and even your happiness—in the future. .

_____

_____

_____

_____

_____

_____

_____

Ride the Waves of Emotions and Cravings

At this point, we hope you are convinced that improving how you cope with emotions is closely associated with stopping binge eating and with overall well-being. Rather than denying, escaping, or avoiding difficult emotions, use the knowledge and tools you've gained this week to face and manage distress.

Below is an effective emotion management plan to use when you face a negative emotion or craving, as outlined in the chapter. The first plan is filled out as an example.

Ride the Waves of Emotions

Worksheet Plan Example

Label it	
Labeling emotions can decrease their intensity.	I am feeling angry.
	My body is tense.
Check your thoughts, body, and behaviors for clues when emotions are hard to identify.	I can't stop thinking about all the possible reasons why my friend lied to me—and what I want to do and say.
Naming your emotions can help you feel better.	

Lean in

Accept all of your emotions. It is impossible not to experience emotions. Even negative emotions have a purpose.	Pretending I'm not angry won't work—it never really does. I have the urge to binge eat. Fantasizing about a binge gives me temporary relief. I have the thought, "I might as well give up because my friend must not care." I also have the urge to call my friend and say mean things. Noticing this anger is a choice point. I know it has a purpose. I will pause before taking any action toward myself and my friend. I don't want to make it worse.

Learn to respond with effective emotion regulation skills

Write expressively Reach out to people Rely on facts for motivation Promote positive emotions with positive coping statements Empower your healthy self Find comforts Engage in positive activities and distractions Take opposite actions	I will reach out to my brother for support rather than get stuck in negative emotions and thought loops or follow my urges. I will seek comfort by getting out in nature for a brisk walk. I'll wait until my anger is less intense before having a conversation with my friend. When we talk about the situation I will use opposite actions by staying curious and compassionate instead of accusatory and harsh. I won't act impulsively, I will focus on how this anger has a purpose—it reveals that I care about myself and want to effectively communicate my needs with others. And, it may be an opportunity to better understand my friend. I know food can't solve this problem so I won't eat to numb, escape, or avoid. I'll empower my healthy self by treating myself the way I would tell a friend to treat themselves in the same situation. That means sticking with my schedule of meals and snacks, without skipping any or eating in between.

Successfully ride the waves of emotions and cravings

Emotional management tools work and can lead to great benefits.

There is space between emotions and actions.

The choice points that exist in that space are powerful and empowering.

Effective coping increases your potential for emotional control, self-confidence, healthy relationships, and reaching goals, and decreases the risk of binge eating and impulsive reactions.

Anger has been hard for me to deal with in the past. It makes me want to do something to numb, avoid, or escape it. This time I took positive actions. Seeking support, comfort, and using opposite action flipped my perspective and brought me a much better outcome. No binge. No shame. No blowup with my friend and no self-sabotage. It took effort not to default to old reactions, but it's worth it.

I gained confidence that I can handle difficult emotions and situations. I stayed true to my health goals!

On the following pages, complete your own plan. Write out an example of an instance when you used effective emotional coping. Refer to the example we provide above for help if you get stuck. Use this worksheet in the future when you are at the height of an intense emotion. Simply download the worksheet at any time from http://www.newharbinger.com/43614. It can be your guide for following through as you build these essential skills.

Ride the Waves of Emotions: Worksheet Plan

Label it

Labeling emotions can decrease their intensity.	_____
	_____
Check your thoughts, body, and behaviors for clues when emotions are hard to identify.	_____
	_____
Naming your emotions can help you feel better.	_____
	_____
	_____

Lean in

Accept all of your emotions.	_____
It is impossible not to experience emotions.	_____
Even negative emotions have a purpose.	_____
	_____
	_____
	_____
	_____

Learn to respond with effective emotion regulation skills

Write expressively

Reach out to people

Rely on facts for motivation

Promote positive emotions with positive coping statements

Empower your healthy self

Find comforts

Engage in positive activities and distractions

Take opposite actions

_____

_____

_____

_____

_____

_____

Successfully ride the waves of emotions and cravings

Emotional management tools work and can lead to great benefits.

There is space between emotions and actions.

The choice points that exist in that space are powerful and empowering.

Effective coping increases your potential for emotional control, self-confidence, healthy relationships, and reaching goals, and decreases the risk of binge eating and impulsive reactions.

_____

_____

_____

_____

_____

_____

Track Your Emotions for Six Days

To consolidate what you've learned about handling your emotions, track your feelings, along with the emotional tools that you found most helpful. Be aware of and name your feelings for the next six days—in the morning and evening. Complete the chart below daily. If you wish to continue tracking for a longer period, you can download blank worksheets at http://www.newharbinger.com/43614.

Day and time	What am I feeling?	What is the situation?	Did I experience an urge to binge eat? Circle Yes or No	List the emotional tools you tried and found effective.
Day 1 Time:			Yes No	
Day 2 Time:			Yes No	
Day 3 Time:			Yes No	

		Yes	No		

Day 4

Time:

		Yes	No		

Day 5

Time:

		Yes	No		

Day 6

Time:

Q&A with Katy Jakle, PsyD

As a compassion-focused psychologist, what do you think are the benefits that can come from making improvements in handling emotions?

One of the great benefits that clients get from making improvements in handling emotions is a greater sense of themselves and who they are in the world. Emotions truly communicate to us what we care about at a fundamental level.

For example, if one of my great values in life is being a present and caring family member, then when it comes to my family I feel grief and sadness related to loss, I feel guilty if I forget an important event, and I feel anxious and fearful if I hear about serious problems or accidents. These emotions, although painful, are not problems. They are normal, human, and necessary.

If clients can experience these emotions as they are, without escalating them or numbing them, then clients will be able to see reality as it is and use this information to organize a thoughtful response.

How can not knowing how to handle the range of our emotions get in the way of experiencing positive emotions?

Clients often come to me with elaborate ways of avoiding emotions or reacting impulsively and ineffectively to their emotions. On either end of the spectrum, these clients are often oscillating between a sense of over- and under-control, and often struggle with decision-making. There is no way to numb out only one part of our emotional experience, such that clients who push away negative emotions lose touch with positive emotions.

What typically underlies our urge to avoid uncomfortable feelings?

A common fear is that looking toward emotional pain will be too overwhelming. This is understandable. These individuals may have seen others act destructively when emotional or may have experienced overwhelming sensations in a situation that led them to fear that pain. Through emotion regulation skills, people learn that emotions in and of themselves can be intense and unpleasant and have behavioral urges—but there are effective skills to respond to them.

Like surfing, we can't control the waves—our immediate, natural emotional experience created through the interaction of our history and biology—but we can learn to surf—our response to that emotional wave. Learning and practicing emotion regulation skills increases our sense of self-efficacy and provides a more realistic sense of what we can truly control: our behavior and our response to emotional experiences.

CHAPTER 8

Week 5: Eating and Living Mindfully

"Ultimately, it is a radical act of sanity and love…
to stop all the doing that carries us through our moments
without truly inhabiting them,
and actually drop into being, even for one fleeting moment."

—Jon Kabat-Zinn

We aren't always aware of what our minds are doing and where our attention is going. If you're like most people (including us authors), you have room for improvement when it comes to being fully present in the moments of your own life. This week, you'll learn about *mindfulness,* the skill of intentionally paying attention to the present moment nonjudgmentally (Kabat-Zinn 2018). It can improve the quality of your life and help with anxiety, sleep, depression, pain, and psychological stress (Lin, Chadi, and Shrier 2019; Hilton et al. 2017; Goyal et al. 2014; Galla et al. 2015). Applying mindfulness can also help you to end your battle with food and overcome mindless, emotional, and binge eating.

Mindfulness may seem vague, mystical, and difficult. In truth, it is unambiguous, ordinary, and simple to learn. Plus, it gets more powerful with practice. Take a moment right now to experience its simplicity with a few moments of mindful sitting:

Sit in a comfortable position with your feet on the floor. Purposely bring your attention to this exact moment. Without using words to label or describe, experience the sensations present in your body. What do you notice? Can you experience how your skin comes into contact with the air? Just observe what you are experiencing.

Once you are fully present in your body, guide your attention to become aware of your surroundings with your senses. Experience any sounds. Take in any smells. Gently pay attention to what you see visually. Notice what it feels like where your feet touch the ground beneath them. Are you aware of any sensations in your hands? Observe any thoughts or emotions that arise as you pay attention to sitting.

If your mind wanders to the past or future, simply return your focus to this exact moment of sitting. At this moment, you are not trying to go anywhere or change anything. Pay attention to being right here, right now. Purposefully bring your attention to the present moment without judging or striving—that is mindfulness.

Key Components of Mindfulness

Mindfulness comprises three main components: purposeful present-moment awareness, a beginner's mind, and nonjudgment (Kabat-Zinn 2012). Let's now look at each one in detail.

Purposeful Present-Moment Awareness

The concept of present-moment awareness in mindfulness refers to what arises as you pay attention. It is not about changing, doing, or striving. Instead, awareness refers to your mind's innate ability to pay attention and be aware of your experience, just as it is now, not as you wish it were. In times when you are emotionally off balance or being pulled in many directions, it takes discipline to intentionally pull your mind back to a state of awareness through sustained attention. Jon Kabat-Zinn describes why awareness is important: "If we are not careful, it is all too easy to fall into becoming more of a human doing than a human being, and forget who is doing all the doing and why" (2012, 18).

> *"I concentrated on listening to my body, taking breaths, and being conscious of those breaths—identifying when discomfort is impending and not allowing myself to recklessly devour through these signs."* —Oliver

Two mental habits that may take you away from present-moment awareness are *multitasking* and *continuous partial attention* (Stone 2009). You're multitasking when switching between two tasks for the sake of potential efficiency, such as cooking while watching a game on TV. You're engaging in continuous partial attention when doing one activity while vigilantly scanning for something better, such as listening to a lecture while checking social media. Not only has cognitive science shown that task switching slows our responses and makes us more error prone (Monsel 2003), it may also be associated with a lack of fulfillment, stress-related problems, and overstimulation (Stone 2009).

Think about how you go about your daily tasks, engage with activities, and spend time with people. Are you usually fully aware of and paying attention to what you are doing, who you are with, and your surroundings? Reflect on your habits of awareness in the past week. Place a check-mark to indicate whether you have been fully present and aware when you engaged in the following activities:

Activity	Fully present and aware	Multitasking or continuous partial attention
Spending time with a friend	☐	☐
Driving	☐	☐
Talking on the phone	☐	☐
Using social media	☐	☐
Working out	☐	☐
Listening to music	☐	☐
Working	☐	☐
Studying	☐	☐
Getting ready for work or school	☐	☐
Engaging in a hobby	☐	☐
Watching TV or a movie	☐	☐
Spending time with animals	☐	☐
Eating	☐	☐
Spending time in nature	☐	☐
Brushing teeth	☐	☐
Washing the dishes	☐	☐
Getting gas	☐	☐

Listening to a lecture or concert	☐	☐
Riding in an elevator	☐	☐
Having your hair cut	☐	☐
Cooking	☐	☐
Putting away laundry	☐	☐
Paying bills	☐	☐

When you review the list above, what do you notice about your tendencies to be fully aware or partially aware? Are you surprised and maybe a little disappointed by how frequently you are not paying attention fully? Choose one activity from this list that you would benefit from engaging in more mindfully in the future. Write down the potential positive impact.

_____

_____

_____

_____

Example: I'd like to be more mindful when I spend time with friends. It's embarrassing when I can't remember what someone has told me because I wasn't listening. When I'm really there with full attention, we have more fun together and our conversations are more interesting.

Practice being in the present-moment mode this week. Choose a time to purposefully pay attention to the experience of eating, rather than task switching or engaging in a distraction:

_____ .

Then follow the directions for the following mindful eating exercise.

Eating Meditation

Being present with your experiences of taste, hunger, fullness, and satisfaction decreases impulsivity with food and lowers the risk of binge eating (Kristeller et al. 2014). Conversely, mindless eating is associated with more frequent emotional eating, responding to cravings and urges, and eating in the absence of hunger. Learning the skill of mindful eating is the practice of slowing down, being fully aware of the eating experience, and noticing satisfaction. The goal is to bring more intentionality to your eating.

1. Choose a single piece of food that is easy to eat, such as a grape, chocolate kiss, cracker, or raisin.

2. Look at the food. Notice its color, size, and shape.

3. Smell the food, notice its scent.

4. Touch the food, notice its texture.

5. Place a piece of the food in your mouth. For one minute, gently move it around in your mouth without chewing or swallowing—from resting on your tongue to touching the roof and sides of your mouth. Be aware of how it feels.

6. Notice the taste. Is it sweet, sour, bitter, salty, savory?

7. Pay attention to the experience of this food without descriptive labels.

8. Slowly, chew the food or allow it to melt. When you're ready, swallow it.

9. Notice, without judgment, any thoughts, feelings, and sensations that arise.

10. Repeat all steps three times with the same food.

Reflect on your experience. Was the last piece of food as pleasurable as the first? What thoughts, feelings, and sensations arose when you experimented with mindful eating?

_____

_____

_____

_____

A Beginner's Mind

The concept of a beginner's mind refers to the attitude of meeting each moment as unknown, fresh, and interesting. Children have this attitude. They are curious about the world. They ask questions and use imaginative play to narrate creative possibilities. As we get older, our life experiences offer us shortcuts to help us build on what we have learned so that we don't repeatedly make the same mistakes. Unfortunately, our knowledge from the past can interfere with our creativity and openness. Zen Master Suzuki Roshi's famous description conveys the importance of this attitude: "In the beginner's mind, there are many possibilities, but in the expert's there are few" (Kabat-Zinn 2012, 9).

You can always choose to reconnect with your beginner's mind. Try to listen more closely. See more clearly. Be curious, awed, and inspired. If you get caught up in hardened ideas, expectations, or rigidity, use this childlike view in your day-to-day life to create more mental space and widen your experiences.

Choose an activity from the list at the beginning of this chapter and, within the next twenty-four hours, try it using a beginner's mind. First, write out your plan. Which activity will you engage in with this childlike perspective? Decide when you'll try it and how you will be curious and open-minded instead of knowing.

_____

_____

_____

_____

Example: Tonight when I stop at the market to get dinner preparations, I will ask myself what foods will satisfy me, what nutrition my body needs. I'll try to be aware of my hunger cues. I am curious what will happen when I thoughtfully tune in—rather than stick with the meal I think I should have or default to what I crave.

After you have tried the activity using a beginner's mind, reflect on your experience of completing an everyday task as if you'd never done it before.

_____

_____

_____

_____

Nonjudgment

The many judgments we make about ourselves and the world take us out of the present moment and often lead to suffering. Think back to recent self-judgments. Perhaps you've told yourself unhelpful food or body image thoughts, or talked yourself out of expanding your relationship circle. Maybe you've said to yourself:

I blew it by eating two doughnuts during my meeting. Now my day is ruined. I should give up eating well.

Dating isn't an option until I change how I look. It's a waste of time to care.

I shouldn't bother joining the soccer team. I'm not the best player and probably won't make friends anyway.

To achieve the nonjudgment aspect of mindfulness, pause when you're being critical and move toward accepting yourself, situations, and people as they are—not as you want them to be. Since you can only be yourself, why not accept who you are without a constant barrage of self-criticism? When you are bored, stressed, or find your mind wandering, resist the temptation to berate yourself and put yourself down. Instead, start a new mental habit: use nonjudgment to treat yourself with kindness.

Build a nonjudgmental stance by practicing *radical acceptance* (Brach 2003):

- Treat your internal experience with understanding, warmth, and friendliness.

- Avoid critical labels for situations, people, your body, and yourself.

- Tolerate emotions, thoughts, and sensations without judgment.

- Accept that everything has a cause.

- Acknowledge that fighting reality won't change it.

- Observe pain; it may be a signal that something is wrong.

- Notice that acceptance may illuminate choices.

"You're already at war with active binge eating, so don't fight it anymore. Instead, develop self-empathy and compassion, just as you would for any child you meet. When you stab yourself with reactive comments of self-hate and despair, learn understanding and compassion for that judgmental, lost warrior one minute at a time. Keep circling back to your self-compassion, your self-empathy." —Charlotte

Complete the chart below to move from a stance of self-criticism to one of nonjudgment. First, choose three times from the past week when you were critical with yourself. Then, in the first column, describe what happened. In the second column, take steps toward radical acceptance and nonjudgment by answering each writing prompt. Take your time with this exercise. You'll need to use mental flexibility to get out of the shame spiral caused by the self-criticism (and binge eating) and to purposefully choose nonjudgment.

Three self-critical events	Steps to radical acceptance and nonjudgment
What happened?	The facts of the situation: My thoughts in that moment: The evidence that my thoughts were true: A nonjudgmental statement to myself that is understanding, warm, and friendly: If I radically accept the situation and myself, what might change?

Three self-critical events	Steps to radical acceptance and nonjudgment
What happened?	The facts of the situation: My thoughts in that moment: The evidence that my thoughts were true: A nonjudgmental statement to myself that is understanding, warm, and friendly: If I radically accept the situation and myself, what might change?

Three self-critical events	Steps to radical acceptance and nonjudgment
What happened?	The facts of the situation: My thoughts in that moment: The evidence that my thoughts were true: A nonjudgmental statement to myself that is understanding, warm, and friendly: If I radically accept the situation and myself, what might change?

Example:

What happened?	The facts of the situation:
Last night, after dinner, I was full. Then I attended an event. I was uncomfortable talking to strangers, so I ate to avoid feeling anxious. My eating was compulsive. When I got home, I was disgusted with myself and then I binged. I felt like a failure and weak. I decided to give up working on this non-diet plan and start a diet instead.	I felt uncomfortable at an event. I ate beyond fullness then binged.

My thoughts in that moment:

I should give up. I have no self-control. The rest of today doesn't matter. I am a failure. This is hopeless so I might as well binge eat. A diet will make me feel better.

The evidence that my thoughts were true:

These thoughts are not true.

The truth is, I can get stronger. Sometimes I already am. The rest of the day matters. Telling myself to binge because it doesn't matter is what I tell myself when I don't want to face reality. I can accept that sometimes I might overeat. I use positive self-control often but am not perfect. Failing today doesn't make me a failure even when I feel awful. I feel even worse after binge eating than I would have if I stopped after eating more than I planned to. Dieting is tempting but never helps me in the long run. Binge eating makes me miserable. I want to stop. Practicing skills can help.

A nonjudgmental statement to myself that is understanding, warm, and friendly:

I can learn better strategies to handle uncomfortable social situations in the future. It's normal to overeat sometimes. I can't expect myself to be perfect. I can give myself grace. It's okay. I'm okay. I fell but I will get back up.

If I radically accept the situation and myself, what might change?

I accept that mistakes happen on the path to success. Even though they hurt, my failures are a chance to get stronger, better, and wiser. I will take time to notice small steps of progress and remember other difficult goals I have reached. Many people have stopped binge eating. I can too. I won't use difficult situations as a reason to eat or sabotage my relationships or my goals. I can be healthy and happy.

Mindfulness and Eating

Mindfulness can help you modify how you eat and help to end your struggle with food (Kristeller and Bowman 2015). Mindfulness can increase your awareness and enable you to respond to internal, rather than external, cues to eat (Warren, Smith, and Ashwell 2017; Katterman et al. 2014). In one twelve-week study of mindfulness-based treatment for binge eating, more than two-thirds of participants no longer met criteria for the disorder at the follow-up four months later (Kristeller and Hallett 1999). The amount of mindfulness practice the participants engaged in was a strong predictor of who improved the most from the treatment. It is noteworthy that this mindfulness-based approach was effective regardless of participants' psychosocial or ethnic backgrounds and religious beliefs or practices.

Mindfulness can also enhance your ability to pay attention to your overall food intake, manage binge triggers, and respond to physical cues of hunger and satiety. In one study, eighteen participants decreased the frequency and size of binges by more than half in just a few weeks of practicing mindfulness (Kristeller and Hallett 1999). In another study, participants who practiced mindfulness for ten weeks found it easier to make food choices based on their nutritional needs, experienced greater pleasure from eating, significantly decreased overeating, and reported less stress about food (Kristeller and Wolever 2014).

"Love yourself. I know it's cliché, but really, really find a way to accept and respect yourself. I am at a place now where I am so sad for the person I was for so many years while bingeing. I made poor decisions because I was looking to external people, things, places, jobs, et cetera to find joy. It did not work. Do not move houses or states or countries as a catalyst to get healthy. Find peace with yourself. Find a way to be so in the moment that you can't help but make choices that serve your strength. You deserve that." —Isaiah

Mindful eating reduces bingeing because it can help you experience more pleasure as you cultivate awareness of taste, choose your portions based on energy needs and satisfaction, and get out of the diet-binge eating cycle. One of us (Gia) co-taught a class on body image and nutrition at UCLA for more than five years. For one assignment, students engaged in a mindful Intuitive Eating experiment (Tribule and Resch 2017). They planned a time to eat their favorite food mindfully, made predictions, and took notes on their present-moment awareness before, during, and after eating. When students discussed their results in class, it was interesting to hear how mindful awareness impacted eating experiences. Some students noticed that their pleasure had faded by the time they paused in the middle of eating their favorite food—some stopped when they noticed it and others kept going. Some students noticed that they didn't enjoy the food as much as they predicted. Others reported they didn't feel well after eating. Some commented on how paying attention helped them experience the pleasure of their favorite food. Some students felt more satisfied than usual.

When you practice mindful eating, you might learn more about what you enjoy, how different foods feel in your body, and the energy you derive from them. You might notice how your preferences and choices change over time.

Using mindfulness to heal your eating problems emphasizes awareness of nutrition, your body, and self-acceptance. For the remainder of this chapter, we will describe methods of mindfulness meditations and mindful eating practices. Using these practices can reduce the number and intensity of binge eating episodes, and it also improves your attitude about eating.

Mindfulness Meditations

Non-eating meditations have been proven to reduce binge eating, emotional eating (Katterman et al. 2014), and binge eating urges (Kristeller and Hallett 1999). The goal of this meditation is to learn to develop a greater capacity to engage your purposeful attention, use detached awareness, and nonjudgmentally observe the sensations of your body and content of your mind.

"Breathing exercises—and exercising in general—helps me vent and redirect my emotions in a healthier fashion." —Oliver

General Meditation

Focus your attention on your breath, which is life-affirming and ever-present. It is also relatively easy not to judge your breath. Remember, the goal is not to relax or to clear your mind—it is just to be present with whatever your experience is and to make a conscious choice to return to observing the breath when you are distracted or resisting. Once you can pay attention to your breath and what arises, you'll be better able to pay attention to any object without judgment and stay present in your body with greater stability.

1. Set a pleasant-sounding timer for twenty minutes. Sit in a relaxed, comfortable position.

2. Close your eyes lightly or keep them open while gently focusing on something in the room.

3. Begin to notice your breath as it comes in through your nose, filling your chest and stomach. Take a small pause at the top of the inhale. Then slowly exhale. Pay attention to the full expanse of each breath going out, and pause again at the bottom of the out-breath. Like waves in the ocean, observe that your inhale and exhale are effortless.

4. Notice any thoughts, emotions, and sensations that arise, without judgment. Pay attention to the present moment, your emotions, sensations in your body, and thoughts in your mind. Be curious, kind, and nonjudgmental.

5. As you notice your breath, try making your exhale one or two counts longer than your inhale. This pattern can be physiologically calming.

6. If you notice moments of resisting this meditation, observe your own resistance. Notice what happens to your resistance when you pay attention to it. Does it soften? Does it expand?

7. Each time you notice that your attention has wandered—which will happen quite a lot!—say yes to paying attention to your breath and then gently guide your mind back.

8. When the timer goes off, open your eyes and begin to come back into the room, open and close your hands, and wiggle your toes. Take a few minutes to reorient yourself.

Reflect on your experience. What was it like to meditate on your breath from moment to moment, to be gently aware, to observe and pay attention to what arises without judgment?

_____

_____

_____

_____

_____

Are you willing to practice this general meditation every day for one week to see the benefits?

Yes   No

If yes, that's great. If doing so seems too difficult, don't give up all together. You might try it for ten minutes rather than twenty. Or try an equally beneficial alternative: a guided meditation. You may find it's easier to meditate with someone guiding you. Look online for free meditations, such as those offered on the website for UCLA's Mindfulness Awareness Research Center, or use an app like Insight Timer.

Choose where and when you'll meditate daily this week: _____

Brief Meditation Breaks

Use this practice to tune in to your mind and body's internal cues, bring present moment-to-moment awareness to all activities, and respond intentionally (rather than react impulsively) to environmental and emotional triggers. Incorporating brief meditations into your daily life can increase your ability to notice the contents of your mind, respond to binge eating triggers more thoughtfully (Kristeller et al. 2014), reduce impulsivity, and develop self-regulation (Lin et al. 2019). The goal is to be present, to not restrict, and to not disconnect from fullness. Engage in this short meditation check-in throughout the day and before all meals and snacks.

1. Stop what you are doing.

2. With your eyes open or closed, purposefully breathe in and out a few times slowly.

3. Pay attention to what is happening in your body.

4. Notice your thoughts and feelings.

5. Observe what is going on around you.

6. Pay attention to your breath coming and going for one to three minutes.

7. Be aware of what matters to you in this moment. You might say to yourself, *I want to nourish my body.*

8. Return to the present moment and respond to the situation mindfully, without reacting.

Reflect on your experience.

_____

_____

_____

_____

_____

_____

Mindful Eating Practices

The mindfulness meditations you have been practicing can help you become less impulsive and reactive in a variety of challenging situations, including when you eat. The following mindfulness practices can further transform how you connect with your body and interact with food. Below are three effective mindful eating skills to support your new non-diet healthy eating habits: experiencing satisfaction from the taste and quality of food, tuning in to your body's internal compass, and facing urges without giving in to them.

QUALITY OVER QUANTITY

Purposeful awareness of taste, satisfaction, and the quality of food can change your internal conversation from one about filling up to one about fueling up (Kristeller et al. 2014) and enjoying flavor-rich foods (Kristeller and Bowman 2015). Observe how you feel in your body and mind after eating and ask yourself questions such as: *Do I have mental energy? Physical energy? Which flavors do I enjoy and how long do they last? How do I experience the benefits of nutrition?* Sometimes you might choose to eat something your body does not need from a nutritional standpoint—and that's okay, because suppressing what brings you pleasure may lead to losing control with that food. As you become more aware of the quality of your food—the flavors, the pleasure, and the energy you experience—notice how your taste buds respond too. After relatively small portions of highly processed foods, your taste buds may decrease their sensitivity. If so, you may get maximum taste satisfaction from purposefully paying attention to those first few bites. But begin to choose foods based on the energy you feel after eating them, the nutrition your body needs to function well, and taste satiety. You can change what is rewarding when you eat by paying purposeful attention to quality over quantity.

This skill focuses on sensory awareness:

- Tuning in to taste

- Enjoying what you eat

- Noticing the foods that nourish and energize you

- Enhancing satisfaction with smaller portions

- Decreasing emotional and binge eating

Choose one meal or snack for taste, nourishment, and enjoyment. Whether you decide to eat a crisp apple, a bowl of pasta, or a handful of sunflower seeds, notice how your taste buds come alive then decrease their sensitivity. Notice how some foods add to your vitality.

1. Portion out a serving. Note: If you are eating a triggering food that you have frequently lost control with in the past, eat with a friend or in a public setting when you have a limited amount of time.

2. Give yourself permission to eat slowly and enjoy your food.

3. Accept that you can eat for the pleasure of taste and quality rather than quantity.

4. Pay attention to the present moment without judgment.

5. Engage your beginner's mind as if you don't know anything about this food.

6. Notice that experiences of taste, pleasure, satisfaction, and energy are rewarding.

Reflect on your experience.

_____

_____

_____

_____

_____

_____

PHYSICAL VERSUS EMOTIONAL OR ENVIRONMENTAL HUNGER CUES

The purpose of this skill is to be able to distinguish between physiological hunger and hunger prompted by emotions or the environment. Start building this skill by bringing a beginner's mind to your hunger and fullness cues, which can be a mix of internal experiences. These internal experiences can include body sensations, energy level, mood, and thoughts. Begin to notice when your body tells you that it's time to start and stop eating.

Read the descriptions of hunger and fullness in the chart that follows (Omichinski 1996; Tribole and Resch 2017). In the third column, write "start" next to the internal experience that best describes when you usually begin eating, and write "stop" next to the experience that best describes when you usually finish eating. In the fourth column, note how often—rarely, daily, weekly, or monthly—you experience each level of hunger and fullness.

Level of physiological hunger	Corresponding internal experience	When do you start or stop?	How often? Rarely, daily, weekly, or monthly?
7 – Too hungry	headache, dizziness, difficulty concentrating, lack of energy, anxious to eat, extreme hunger		
6 – Very hungry	irritability, low energy, uncomfortable stomach, nausea, moderate hunger		
5 – Comfortably hungry	stomach feels a bit empty, desire to eat, waning energy, mild hunger		
4 – Satisfied	body sensations of satisfaction, absence of hunger, neutral, fueled		
3– Comfortably full	stomach has room for a few more bites, taste buds less sensitive, desire to eat comes from thoughts not body, mild fullness		
2 – Very full	stomach discomfort, sleepy, unpleasantness, distress, past fullness		
1 – Too full	pain, desire to be alone, tiredness, bloating, thoughts of shame, extreme fullness		

Review what you wrote in the chart.

What do you notice about when you usually start and stop eating? Does this habit support peace with food? If not, what can you change?

_____

_____

_____

What do you notice about how frequently you experience extreme levels of hunger and extreme levels of fullness? Does this pattern lead to binge eating? Reflect on what you can change in the future.

_____

_____

_____

Mindfully Respond to Physiological Hunger

Pay attention to your hunger cues. Observe how they show up in your body. You may feel emptiness in your stomach, a slight headache, or a dip in energy. Or you may notice that you become impatient or that your concentration wavers. Whatever you notice, just observe it without judgment.

Resist any temptation to ignore sensations of *comfortable hunger,* even if you think, *I shouldn't be hungry.* Your hunger cues are life preserving, and if you get *too hungry,* you are likely to seek out unbalanced meals or to overeat.

In addition, check in with your body's cues—your built-in compass—to investigate where they are coming from. Are your thoughts or urges to eat being triggered by the environment or emotions in the absence of physiological hunger? If you aren't experiencing hunger sensations in your body, wait until you do before eating. Leave self-judgment behind and adopt a beginner's mind when you notice hunger. Eat when you are *comfortably hungry.* Say yes to the reality of the (non-diet-based) balanced nutrition your body needs. Notice the thoughts that arise as you take into account your day's schedule, a gentle inventory of what you've already eaten, and your activity level. Ask yourself whether you've had enough fruits, vegetables, protein, liquids, healthy fats, and starches. If you are feeling impulsive, take a step back. If you have been disconnecting from your body, it's time to reconnect.

1. Notice physical hunger.

2. Begin a meal.

3. Pay attention to the level of your hunger. Accept your hunger level even if you think you should be more or less hungry than you feel.

4. Choose what you will eat through a present-moment awareness of your needs for nutrition, energy, pleasure, and satiety.

5. Without judgment, eat to satisfy your physical hunger.

Reflect on your experience.

_____

_____

_____

_____

_____

_____

BUILD A COMPASS FOR STOMACH-FULLNESS CUES

Use a beginner's mind to purposefully pay attention to how and when you experience fullness during meals. Observe your body's sensations as you eat. Stop eating when you are satisfied or comfortably full. It is common—but not helpful—to eat past fullness or begin eating when you are full. If you tend to push past being satisfied and resist noticing fullness or resist stopping in response, you may be out of contact with your internal cues (Kristeller and Bowman 2015). As you pay attention, you may notice that you feel satisfied after less food than you'd expect, or you may need to eat more than you expect. Don't judge your internal compass; respect it. This is an essential skill as you make peace with food.

"My dietician gave me no specific diet, no restrictions. Every time I'd meet with her I'd say, 'So, I should probably not eat cake, right?' And she'd say, 'No, that's fine.' To everything. Everything. I didn't trust her for a long time. But I followed her meal plan—which was a lot of food. And you know what? I was full all the time. I never went hungry. I could eat basically whatever I wanted. And eventually, I stopped restricting—which led to no more bingeing." —Mia

Practice paying attention to your body's experience of fullness at one meal to develop a compass that cues your mind to stop eating based on your body's sensations. Learn to notice the difference. What is neutral, comfortable fullness, and intense fullness?

1. Begin a meal.

2. Stay present with any thoughts, feelings, and sensations that arise.

3. Pause when you have eaten 50 percent. Tune in to your body to notice your present-moment level of fullness.

4. Pause again at 75 percent. Tune in to your body to notice your level of fullness.

5. Become aware of how you notice feeling satisfied. What cues is your body giving you? Some people notice taking a deep breath as they reach stomach fullness.

6. When you reach a comfortable, gentle level of fullness, let that signal the end of your meal. Stop eating.

Reflect on your experience.

_____

_____

_____

_____

_____

SURF THE URGE

Paradoxically, accepting that experiencing cravings and urges is beyond your control can improve your ability to gain control over them. A study of undergraduates (Forman et al. 2007) separated participants into groups. Each person was asked to carry around boxes of chocolates for forty-eight hours without eating any. To handle the cravings, one group was given the instructions to accept the cravings and urges, the other was told to try to control them. Results showed that accepting them led to greater abstinence from eating the chocolates, especially for participants who tended to be most challenged by cravings.

Surfing the urge (Bowen and Marlatt 2009) is a strategy that can help curb cravings. Basically, you treat the urge like a wave that gets bigger before it crashes on shore and dissipates.

1.   The next time you experience a craving or urge, notice it in the present moment.

2.   Without judgment, accept the experience as beyond your control.

3.   Take a step back. Observe yourself having the urge or craving.

4.   Be willing to experience it—to surf the urge—as it comes and goes.

5.   Set a timer for thirty minutes and commit to not taking any action for at least that amount of time.

6.   Say yes to focusing on an alternative thought, feeling, or activity. Pay attention on purpose.

7.   If your mind wanders back to the urge, simply return your focus to the distracting activity.

8.   If the urge is intense, try placing your attention on your breath coming and going. You can think of your breath as the surfboard helping you ride that urge to shore.

Reflect on your experience.

_____

_____

_____

_____

_____

Mindfulness offers proven strategies to help end your struggle with food and to improve your health. Remember, applying present-moment awareness, a beginner's mind, and nonjudgment will also help you feel more at ease with yourself. You may begin to tune in to satisfaction and reconnect with your body. The goal is to accept what you enjoy and meet your body's needs.

You can begin to pause and purposefully respond rather than react when you're feeling overwhelmed or experiencing a craving. You can start to be with yourself, other people, and in your surroundings more intentionally. The purpose of mindfulness is to grow your capacity for selecting where you focus your attention—to say yes on purpose. The more you practice, the more benefits you will reap!

Q&A with J. Greg Serpa, PhD

What does mindfulness mean to you as a mindfulness teacher and trainer?

Mindfulness means paying exquisite attention to the experiences of the present moment with kindness and curiosity.

How does mindfulness help us?

As you cultivate the capacity to "be with" experience, you can move from *reacting* automatically when facing challenging emotions or events to *responding* skillfully. This requires getting close to the workings of your body, mind, and heart, and creating a bit of space to allow things to be just as they are.

Of course, this capacity doesn't make all of our struggles magically disappear! All too often, we contract around a struggle and ruminate about it endlessly. We might magically believe that our lives can only improve when all of our problems are resolved. But please don't wait to live your life until everything is perfect—you might be waiting a long time!

There is always a pothole in the road on life's journey. How we relate to these potholes, however, is something we can do something about. Imagine, for a moment, that all your troubles are a teaspoon of salt. If you put the salt into a glass of water, the water will be unbearably salty. Now imagine you put the same salt into a giant swimming pool of water. The size of the problem is the same but you won't even notice the saltiness.

Our attention works much like this. We contract, in both the mind and the body, when we hit a tough spot. But we can create more spaciousness to hold our experiences with a bit more grace and ease. There will still be challenges, or potholes, or salt, or whatever. But you can relate to it differently, as only one part of your experience. This takes, of course, some practice.

How do you suggest that someone new to mindfulness gets started?

Many communities offer mindfulness-based stress reduction (MBSR) or other mindfulness-based classes. It is helpful to have an experienced teacher, but there are also apps you can download onto your phone. Guided mindfulness audio tracks are also widely available on the Internet, often for free. You are welcome to download audio files from my website, http://www.SharingMindfulness.com.

Feel free to start simply by just softly closing your eyes and taking four gentle breaths, really paying attention to how it feels to be breathing. Increase your practice to one minute, then five minutes, and maybe twenty minutes over time. Your mind will wander, and thoughts, sensations, and emotions will distract you. That is simply how it is for everyone. Just return, over and over, to the next breath.

Isn't mindfulness just about relaxation?

This is a common misunderstanding. I call this the "fabric softener fallacy"—the incorrect belief that meditation will make everything soft, cuddly, and sweet smelling, just like fabric softener. Wouldn't that be nice! Instead, mindfulness lets us be with experience just as it is. Mindfulness lets us be with *ourselves* just as we are. Very often you might experience boredom, annoyance, heartache, arousal, itchiness, anger, resentment, delight, and every other experience that is available to all of us. But we learn to be with everything with patience and ease and, hopefully, some kindness toward what it is like to live a human life.

CHAPTER 9

Week 6: Cultivate More Satisfying Relationships to Make Peace with Food

*"We are social mammals and could never have survived
without deeply interconnected and interdependent human contact."*

—Bruce Perry

Our desire to connect with others and to belong is universal, fundamental, and hard-wired (Yalom 2009). Many studies confirm that satisfying intimate relationships are an essential condition of happiness and that secure social ties predict health and well-being (Waldinger et al. 2015). In our experience, reducing isolation is one of the most powerful motivators of change for people who want to make peace with food. This week, you'll have the opportunity to zero in on effective techniques that can boost your interpersonal well-being.

Reflect on how satisfied you are with your current relationships. How might your life improve if you felt happier in your relationships?

_____

_____

_____

_____

Reflect on how satisfied you are with your ability to develop new relationships. How might your life improve if you felt more ease in widening your social circle?

_____

_____

_____

_____

Using research-driven strategies, we will guide you to identify patterns that may be contributing to relationship difficulties and to learn skills to build the kind of relationships you want. Becoming more interpersonally competent, supported, and connected is one of the most powerful research-backed interventions for reducing binge eating behaviors (Hilbert and Tuschen-Caffier 2005).

Interpersonal psychotherapy was developed to improve interpersonal functioning as a mechanism for expanding social support, bringing about positive changes in ongoing relationships, and resolving symptoms. There is solid evidence that when people with binge eating improve their relationships, they experience two important benefits: improvement in self-esteem and reduction in binge eating symptoms (Weisman, Markowitz, and Klerman 2007).

The Role of Relationships in Binge Eating

There are many influences on the quality of the social networks we weave together as we create a meaningful life. Unfortunately, building and strengthening your relationships may have been compromised if you have been dealing with eating problems for many years. It is possible that the interpersonal issues you found tricky at the developmental stage when your eating problems started may not be the same ones confronting you now. Furthermore, the distress and distraction that accompany binge eating may have reduced your capacity to face and negotiate relationship struggles (Murphy et al. 2012).

Problems with relationships are common for people with eating disorders and seem to be a pathway in maintaining them (Murphy et al. 2012; Leehr et al. 2015). Binge eating may be a maladaptive attempt to manage the stress, sadness, anger, frustration, anxiety, loneliness, and disconnection that may be a result of unsatisfying relationships (Dingemans et al. 2017; Adam and Epel 2007). For example, participants in one study shared that thinking about comfort food reduced feelings of loneliness, and eating comfort food caused them to think about and feel more connected to their relationships (Troisi et al. 2015).

Additionally, when relationship problems cause us to feel bad about ourselves and lead to low self-esteem, binge eating may serve as a temporary respite from our negative self-evaluations (Murphy et al. 2012). However, the upset and shame that follow binge eating intensify patterns of social isolation and low self-esteem (Fairburn et al. 2003; Glasofer et al. 2013).

"Taking stock of the social life and connections I had when I was pretending to not have an eating disorder made me aware of how much richer my life would be without the disorder… There are so many ways that relationships meet my needs now. But because people had let me down at some point in the past, I didn't trust them to meet my needs—and instead used food." —Samuel

The goal of this chapter is to interrupt a negative cycle among relationships, self-esteem, and eating—and to help you feel empowered to ameliorate interpersonal areas where you feel stuck, expand the quality of your relationships, and establish new bonds. The final section of this chapter will be your opportunity to create an action plan for your relationships that can bring you more happiness.

As clinicians, we have observed that when people recover from disordered eating, not only does their eating become more nourishing, flexible, and pleasure-filled, their relationships usually do too. You'll discover that it works in the other direction also: intentionally making relationships more satisfying can help you to stop binge eating.

What Are Your Relational Stuck Points?

Patterns that may be getting you stuck include trouble with a lack of desired closeness, complications of changes, differences in expectations with important others, dealing with loss, and avoidance of meaningful life goals (Murphy et al. 2012). As you make direct improvements in these areas of interpersonal functioning, you should begin to notice positive changes in your relationship with food.

Wanting More Closeness

Difficulty with closeness is the most common interpersonal challenge among people who binge eat (Murphy et al. 2012). Deficits in this area can lead to loneliness, isolation, or a lack of intimate, supportive connections (Weissman et al. 2007).

Is *closeness* a current stuck point for you? Reflect on the following questions. Circle yes or no.

Do you find it hard to consistently establish closeness?	Yes	No
Is it difficult for you to strengthen your connections?	Yes	No
Do you have trouble maintaining satisfying relationships?	Yes	No
Do you frequently feel lonely or isolated?	Yes	No
Do you have difficulty getting support when you need it?	Yes	No
Do you need to learn new skills to improve relationships?	Yes	No
Is it hard to participate in social activities and enjoy them?	Yes	No
Do you have trouble getting along with family members?	Yes	No
Do you often feel misunderstood by others?	Yes	No
Is it hard for you to understand others?	Yes	No

Use the goals in the following table to consider positive changes you can make to increase closeness. Intimacy in relationships can be enhanced by increasing understanding, receiving and giving support, engaging actively in pleasurable activities, and expanding your connections. Reflect on how you can experiment with establishing new relationship patterns that can bring you more closeness, happiness, and well-being.

Read the table. Complete the middle section.

Goals	My plan to improve	Positive impact
I want to...	*Relationship, activity, or situation*	
... feel better understood	Relationship: Step:	• Strengthen and maintain relationships
... understand others better	Relationship: Step:	• Strengthen and maintain relationships
... receive more support	Relationship: Step:	• Strengthen and maintain relationships
... give more support to others	Relationship: Step:	• Strengthen and maintain relationships
... feel less isolated and lonely	Relationship: Step:	• Strengthen and maintain relationships
... build new relationships	Relationship: Step:	• Strengthen and maintain relationships

Moving Through Role Changes and Transitions

It can be difficult to adapt to a new social role brought about by a life transition. Whether the change is positive or negative, role changes can get us stuck because they require us to accept the losses as well as the benefits inherent in these developmental moves (Frank and Levenson 2011).

For example, graduating is positive because it marks an achievement. Yet it may also bring about feelings of loss—of a community, a lifestyle, and a sense of competence. Despite the obvious benefits of heading from one phase of life into another, changes can be challenging. When you navigate these developmental transitions well, it can lead you to feel empowered.

Is a *role change* a current stuck point for you? Reflect on the following questions. Circle yes or no.

Are you having difficulty with a new social role?	Yes	No
Do you have a new job or job title that is challenging?	Yes	No
Do you feel unprepared for being a graduate?	Yes	No
Are you having trouble adjusting to being a retiree?	Yes	No
Is it hard to be in the role of parent or empty nester?	Yes	No
Has a move to a new home, city, or state been difficult?	Yes	No
Is being newly married, divorced, or separated distressing?	Yes	No
Is it difficult to connect with others in your new role?	Yes	No
Do you feel helpless in the new role?	Yes	No
Is it hard to master the new role?	Yes	No

The questions above should raise your awareness about transitions you might be facing as you make a step forward in your life. Use the goals in the worksheet below to process difficulties and benefits of your new situation. Successfully meeting the demands of a developmental transition can make you feel stronger and more confident.

If you are experiencing stuckness due to a *life transition*, read the table below. Complete the middle section.

Goals	My plan to adapt	Positive impact
I want to...		
... accept the loss of my old role	The losses about my old situation...include:	• Accept thoughts and feelings of loss
... evaluate the loss realistically	The positive aspects of leaving my old situation:	• Accept positive thoughts and feelings
... view my new role optimistically	The positive aspects of my new situation:	• Optimism • Accept positive thoughts and feelings
... learn new skills for the new role	Skills I need to learn (over time) to be successful in my new situation:	• Learn • Master • Build competence
... develop new social contacts in my new role	To get connected and feel supported in my new situation, I can take these steps:	• Support • Expand relationships
... notice the possible rewards	The potential rewards that can come from this change are:	• Strengthen relationships • Build confidence

Syncing Expectations with Someone Important

Disputes over roles and expectations can cause difficulty in relationships (Frank and Levenson 2011). Problems may occur if we have an ongoing or intense disagreement about roles that leads to conflict, impasse, or hopelessness with someone important to us.

"It was separating from a toxic relationship, intentionally choosing relationships characterized by kindness, and finding unconditional love that allowed my recovery to be possible." —Hailey

For example, if two people adopt a puppy, they have to think about who will take care of walking, feeding, bathing, training, and vet visits. If they recognize the role-related responsibilities and confront the situation successfully, they may come to a mutually satisfying plan about each person's expectations. On the other hand, if they cannot agree, they may experience strain in their relationship.

Is *syncing expectations* a current stuck point for you? Reflect on the following questions. Circle yes or no.

Are you experiencing a relationship dispute?	Yes	No
Do you feel distressed by nonreciprocal expectations?	Yes	No
Do you ignore people or issues, stay silent, or withdraw?	Yes	No
Have solution-oriented discussions stopped?	Yes	No
Do you feel hopeless about having positive control?	Yes	No
Has a stressful life event led to a conflict?	Yes	No
Does it seem as if you have no options left for resolution?	Yes	No
Is the issue so large that you might you end the relationship?	Yes	No
Is your communication about the dispute very intense?	Yes	No
Are you finding it hard to empathize with each other?	Yes	No

Now that you've answered the questions above, you can identify whether syncing expectations is problematic. It's helpful to recall how you created successful outcomes in similar disputes or relationships. Sometimes confronting disparate expectations may lead to more distance or to the dissolution of a relationship. Notice the goals for getting unstuck in this area.

If you are experiencing difficulty *syncing expectations,* read the table below. Complete the middle section.

Goals	My plan to adapt	Positive impact
I want to…		
… be clear, direct, and assertive about the problem	Our expectations are in conflict. The problem is:	• Accept the dispute • Reduce aggressive or passive approach
… express my wishes and feel less distressed	I will share that my wishes are: I will object to these excessive demands:	• Accept self • Accept boundaries
… modify how I communicate	I will change my tone to be: I will change my language to be: I will change my intensity to be: I will actively listen by:	• Increase empathy • Strengthen and maintain relationships

… move beyond our impasse with new, potential, alternative resolutions	Option 1 Pros: Cons: Option 2 Pros: Cons:	• Build optimism • Think flexibly • Strengthen and maintain relationships
… accept a relationship ending if reconciliation is not possible	I will reach out for support from: I will feel stronger and more resilient when I:	• Accept loss • Expand support • Boost resilience
… improve our harmony	I will keep our happiness and bond in mind by remembering:	• Strengthen and maintain relationships

Dealing with Loss

Grief is normal after the death of a close person. Unfortunately, the onset of eating problems may be associated with a significant or complex loss (Weissman et al. 2007). When we do not progress through mourning or do not reestablish our engagement in interests and relationships, loss can become an interpersonal stuck point.

Is *loss* a current area of stuckness for you? Reflect on the following questions. Circle yes or no.

Have you been avoiding grieving a loss?	Yes	No
Are you avoiding your other existing relationships?	Yes	No
Do you feel hopeless about enjoying new relationships?	Yes	No
Have you stopped participating in past interests?	Yes	No
Are you avoiding activities that could bring you pleasure?	Yes	No

If you are experiencing stuckness due to difficulty with a significant *loss,* read the table below, pay particular attention to the goals, and complete the middle column.

Goals	My plan to adapt	Positive impact
I want to…		
… reach out for support for my grief	I will turn to:	• Accept feelings and thoughts • Build support
… engage in available relationships	To get (re)connected and feel supported, I can take these steps:	• Strengthen, maintain, and expand relationships
… participate in activities	I will participate in something I used to enjoy and something new that interests me:	• Build optimism • Increase opportunity for pleasure • Boost resilience

Build an Effective Relationship Tool Kit

Cultivating supportive, satisfying relationships is a key to happiness—and to peace with food—because we are social beings (Costin and Grabb 2011). Now that you have tackled areas of relational stuckness, let's focus on improving your relationship skills, including being able to:

- Communicate with clarity

- Make choices wisely

Choose one current relationship to keep in mind as you practice the skills you'll learn.

_____

Why is improving this relationship important to you now?

_____

_____

_____

Communicate with Clarity

Communicating more effectively has the potential to significantly change your life for the better! Conversely, negative communication has the potential to cause pain and isolation. You can benefit significantly from improving _how_ you relate and connect: more self-care, more feelings of worthiness, more closeness, more support, more competence, more reciprocity, and more empowerment are all rewards.

First, we'll start with the skills that strengthen your connections indirectly by positively changing how you treat yourself. The remainder will fine-tune how you listen to and share, empathize, and negotiate with important people in your life.

DEVELOP SELF-KINDNESS

Self-kindness is an important interpersonal skill because research shows that people who treat themselves with care and compassion have more satisfying relationships (Neff and Germer 2018). Be curious and honest with yourself. What is your self-talk like when something goes wrong? Do you jump to criticize and judge yourself? Or is your response grounded in gentleness and good will? Are you willing to stop being harsh with yourself?

You can choose to make being your own best friend a habit. Being more supportive of yourself during difficult times can lead you to become more understanding, flexible, and open with others. Self-kindness can also lessen the intensity of your emotional reactions, counter any tendency to avoid problems, and positively impact the tone of your interactions. Are you willing to stop constant self-criticism and self-judgment?

Complete the following sentence:

When I make a mistake, instead of attacking myself, I will approach myself the way I would treat a close friend by saying:

_____

_____

_____

_____

ACCEPT BEING IMPERFECTLY LOVABLE

Being human is inextricably linked to being *imperfect*. It may seem counterintuitive, but cultivating meaningful and lasting relationships partially rests on your willingness to accept that you cannot be perfect. This skill will enable you to more honestly connect with yourself and others while still striving for your best.

In *The Gifts of Imperfection* (2010), author Brené Brown describes how perfectionism hampers growth: "Perfectionism is not the same thing as striving to be your best. Perfectionism is the belief that if we live perfect, look perfect, and act perfect, we can minimize or avoid the pain of blame, judgment, and shame. It's a shield. It's a twenty-ton shield that we lug around thinking it will protect us when, in fact, it's the thing that's really preventing us from flight."

Holding yourself to an unyielding standard of perfection may make you feel unworthy of mutual, enduring relationships and lead you to isolate yourself in an effort to cover up mistakes and vulnerabilities. You can stop the cycle of perfectionism, shame, and isolation. By accepting your missteps and flaws as unavoidable human realities, you'll increase your well-being (Neff and Germer 2018).

Complete the following sentence:

Even though I cannot be perfect, I am worthy of love and respect because:

_____

_____

_____

_____

KNOW THE CHANGES YOU WANT

To build better relationships, you need to notice what you want and share your true self with clarity and directness (Weissman et al. 2007). If you could change anything about the quality of one of your relationships, what would it be? Do you want to have more fun together? Exercise, volunteer, garden, dance, or cook together? Be in more or less daily contact? Talk seriously more or less often?

Your emotions serve as a guide when acting on this skill. When you notice positive or negative emotions that arise in your relationship, you have information about changes you may want.

What do you wish to change in your current relationship? Include your needs and feelings.

_____

_____

_____

_____

SPEAK UP WELL

Once you have identified *what* you want to change, you'll want to enhance *how* you communicate. If speaking up makes you feel uncomfortable, we encourage you to tolerate the discomfort and allow yourself to be known. And in order to be able to speak up effectively, you'll need to improve the quality and quantity of your communications (Frank and Levenson 2011). This starts with refining the skill of assertiveness.

Start by observing your tone and directness. Problems in relationships are unlikely to be well resolved if you or the other person is passive or aggressive (McKay et al. 2007). Avoid both ends of the continuum. Don't withdraw, go silent, or avoid the other person, because those passive behaviors will shut down the process. It's also not helpful to be aggressive; verbal attacking, blaming, yelling, stonewalling, or demeaning will likely make the other person feel psychologically unsafe to share honestly. Negative communication behaviors may interfere in creating empathy as you attempt to negotiate a compromise. Assertiveness is the middle path between passive and aggressive; try to communicate from this stance.

When you speak up assertively, own your feelings and thoughts. Be clear and direct. You can't rely on someone else to read your mind even if you think your reasoning and needs are obvious. Use "I" statements such as "I think," "I want," "I wish," "I need," "I hope," or "I feel" rather than "You should" or "You shouldn't." Try to find a calm time and place for your conversation. Give yourself permission to say no. Saying no to someone else's request for change is not selfish, even if it's a new skill for you. Stay non-blaming as you share your perspective.

What are the changes you'd like in your relationship? Remember to be clear and to use "I" statements.

SHARE KINDNESS

If we want love and respect from others, we have to be willing to offer it (Burns 2008). When you show a positive regard, you provide evidence that you respect and admire others even at times when you're in a difficult situation or feeling unsatisfied.

Complete the following sentence:

When speaking up for the changes I'd like to see in our relationship, I will convey genuine warmth, caring, respect, and admiration by saying:

_____

_____

_____

_____

LISTEN AND VALIDATE WELL

To resolve relationship problems, stay open and expand your capacity to hear someone else's point of view. Here are some tips for improving how you listen to others (Frank and Levenson 2011; McKay et al. 2007):

- Stay calm

- Ask the other person to be clear and direct about their needs, wants, and feelings

- Don't interrupt

- Focus on what they're saying

- Avoid trying to read their mind

- Ask questions

- Pause to take in what you heard prior to planning your response

- Check out the truth of your assumptions

Once you think you truly understand, offer validation by verbally stating what you heard, even if you disagree.

What needs, wants, and feelings has the person in your relationship communicated about a desired change?

_____

_____

_____

_____

SHARE EMPATHY

After speaking up, listening carefully, and validating, you are more likely to have a better understanding of the other person (empathy). When you use these tools, you also give others a chance to accurately understand you. The experience of mutual empathy can enhance your bond and lay the groundwork for more consideration when negotiating changes and compromises.

How might more empathy improve closeness and compromise in your current relationship?

_____

_____

_____

_____

FACE THE FACTS

At this time, what is the challenge in the relationship you most want to improve? Specify what you are confronting and the relevant factors (Weissman et al. 2007). When and how did the problem start? What have you tried already? Is your concern new or long-standing? Do you feel at an impasse? If you are hopeless, do you have the support you need if the relationship ends? What has helped you in similar situations in the past that might help now? Embrace, rather than resist, what's happening.

"My newest thing is pure honesty, no matter what. With everything. Honesty in the moment with how I feel is what keeps me in the moment. No white lies or exaggerations. Nothing but pure me. It is interesting the changes that start to happen around you when you show up in the world present and willing to just be." —Isaiah

How do you define the problem in your relationship? Do you feel hopeful about resolving it?

_____

_____

_____

_____

PREPARE TO DE-ESCALATE

Unfortunately, there are times when trying to solve a problem can make matters worse if emotions become too intense. There are many factors that may lead to an escalation in emotional intensity, such as the nature of the problem, how our role models handled disagreements, and our mood, just to name a few (McKay et al. 2007). Physical and emotional safety are primary. Therefore, in an abundance of caution, make a plan for how you will deal with risky situations.

Strong feelings of anger toward the other person or directed at you, feelings of hopelessness about life, out-of-control yelling, or becoming physical are some of the cues that negotiating should be immediately paused. When strong negative emotions or behaviors start to overwhelm the situation, you may notice your heart pounding, a gut instinct, sweating, muscle tightening, feeling hot, louder voices, an aggressive stance, aggressive behaviors, a loss of control, punishing statements, or bullying behaviors. Be prepared to interrupt any unsafe situation. Take action such as getting to another physical space, taking time out, or reaching out to someone else for support. Once you are at a safe distance, consider spending time with someone comforting, engaging in mindfulness, or getting into nature (just to name a few options) to reduce your physiological arousal. There are times when the best thing you can do is leave.

What steps will you take if negotiating is not emotionally or physically safe?

_____

_____

_____

_____

Once calm is returned, if the relationship is not toxic, identify a time and place to try again.

Make Choices Wisely

Even if you are at an impasse or feel hopeless about finding a solution to an interpersonal challenge you're facing, there are alternatives you may have not considered (Frank and Levenson 2011). Maybe you have inadvertently become cognitively rigid and feel trapped by right-or-wrong, should-or-shouldn't, good-or-bad, or all-or-nothing thoughts. Let's practice flexible thinking, creating alternatives, and making wise decisions.

Below are relationship goals you might want to consider as you practice wise decision-making. This list is meant to spark your imagination but not limit you. Check off ones that apply.

☐ Better communication

☐ More emotional, verbal, or physical intimacy

☐ Less conflict

☐ More empathy

☐ Align expectations

☐ End a toxic relationship

☐ Increase participation in shared interests

☐ Cultivate new relationships

☐ Ask for more support

☐ Adapt better to a life transition

☐ More openness to activities

☐ More satisfaction overall

☐ _____

☐ _____

Now consider one problem in one of your relationships. Describe that change you want to see, then generate three potential solutions to help you reach your relationship goal. Consider the consequences each may lead to. Complete each sentence below. An example follows.

A change I want to make in an important relationship is: _____

_____

_____

_____

Potential solution 1: _____

_____

_____

_____

Potential *positive* outcome: _____

_____

_____

_____

Potential *negative* outcome: _____

_____

_____

_____

Potential solution 2: _____

_____

_____

_____

Potential *positive* outcome: _____

_____

_____

_____

Potential *negative* outcome: _____

_____

_____

_____

Potential solution 3: _____

_____

_____

_____

Potential *positive* outcome: _____

_____

_____

_____

Potential *negative* outcome: _____

_____

_____

_____

Compare the possible consequences you generated. When viewed realistically and based on your relationship goal, which is most likely to lead to the greatest happiness for you?

The wise solution I will choose is:

_____

_____

I believe it will lead to more happiness because:

_____

_____

_____

Example:

A change I want to make in an important relationship is: Get closer. I want to travel together like we used to. I feel closer to my partner when we are away from home, work, and our responsibilities. The adventure of traveling and time to relax refreshes me too. It makes me feel energized to take better care of myself and to be a better partner.

Potential solution 1: Take two weeklong trips a year to places we both want to visit. Start budgeting and planning.

Potential positive outcome: We feel excited about having travel time together on the calendar. It's fun to plan.

Travel and exploring bring us closer.

Potential negative outcome: We may not have the time or money to get away for two weeklong trips every year.

Potential solution 2: We can plan two shorter trips.

Potential positive outcome: *Save money when it's tight. Get away when longer trips are hard to fit in. We feel excited about having travel time together on the calendar. It's fun to plan. Travel, exploring bring us closer.*

Potential negative outcome: *It's not as exciting, bonding, or relaxing when we take shorter trips.*

Potential solution 3: *We plan one day every month to try something new and set our responsibilities aside. We can tell family, friends, and work that we are "away." We take turns planning the day.*

Potential positive outcome: *We feel excited about having our days on the calendar. We don't have to wait so long to have quality time together. It's easy to budget the time and money.*

Potential negative outcome: *We might make excuses or cancel more easily because our day together doesn't involve travel. Others might not take our boundary seriously.*

Compare the possible consequences you generated. When viewed realistically and based on your relationship goal, which is most likely to lead to the greatest happiness for you? The wise solution I will choose is: *#3. This option balances closeness and relaxation with current constraints: budget for travel, not being far from home, exploring brings us close, easy to get backup help to be "away" for one day at a time. I believe it will lead to the most happiness because it is the least stressful while also achieving the goal.*

Keep Happiness and Well-Being in Mind

To recap, clinical experience and research show that enhancing your relational life can positively impact your eating and well-being. Therefore, we want you to transform the knowledge you gained this week into an action plan. Increasing your competence can help you to strengthen and sustain your current relationships, and feel empowered to reach out and develop new relationships.

> *"The few therapists I saw that 'got it' were important, as well as a nonjudgmental, non-diet-following, size-accepting community. The role of that community was one of the biggest impacts in finding recovery and sustaining it."* —Chloe

Using what you have learned about your relationship stuck points and the interpersonal tool kit, complete the Positive Relationships Plan on the following page. Remember that being connected with others can improve your life. Supportive, satisfying relationships can increase your self-esteem, decrease binge eating, and expand your happiness!

Positive Relationships Plan

The action I will take to make one current relationship closer is: _____

_____

_____

_____

The action I will take to strengthen or maintain one of my current relationships is: _____

_____

_____

_____

The action I will take to improve how I handle the relationship I have with myself is: _____

_____

_____

_____

The action I will take to reach out for support about a relationship difficulty I am facing is: ___

_____

_____

_____

The action I will take to build new connections is: _____

_____

_____

_____

CHAPTER 10

Week 7: Choose to Improve Your Environment

"Design your life to minimize reliance on willpower."

— B. J. Fogg

Have you ever found yourself heading to your usual parking spot, only to arrive and remember that you parked somewhere different that day? Or found yourself taking your typical route home, and later remembering that you were supposed to make an important detour along the way? Many of our behaviors happen on autopilot, shaped by habit and environmental cues that are outside of conscious awareness (Marteau, Hollands, and Fletcher 2012). Just like it can be hard to remember deviations from your normal routine for heading home, habits and subtle prompts from the environment can make it difficult to change your eating patterns and stop bingeing.

In this chapter, you will learn to identify the environmental cues that trigger your binge eating and develop counteracting strategies to help you maintain the progress you're making.

The Modern Food Environment

Part of why it's so difficult to stop binge eating is the mismatch between the environment in which our bodies and brains developed and the world in which we currently live (Hall 2016). For most of human evolution, calorie-dense foods were relatively scarce and required time and energy to find. Humans developed a hardwired preference for fats and sugars that helped our ancestors get the motivation to seek out these rare but important foods. That was great for the survival of the species, but it has created problems for humans living in the modern world, where calorie-dense foods are plentiful and easily accessible.

Gone are the days when we expended a great deal of energy hunting for or farming our own food. Using new technologies, food scientists create foods that specifically exploit the natural human desire for the taste of fat, sugar, and salt. Moreover, reminders about these foods are everywhere, from billboards along our commutes to the televisions inside our homes. This mismatch between the environment in which our food preferences evolved and the reality of our modern food landscape has made following through with healthy eating intentions challenging. Because of the way the outside world is engineered to encourage overeating, it is vitally important to design your personal environment and routines to counteract those urges and promote healthy behaviors.

Environments That Trigger Binges

In addition to the challenges posed by the outside world, additional risk for binges can come from the way that we construct our personal environments and routines. In this section, you will learn to identify some of the most common environmental triggers for binge eating and develop a plan to combat them.

Personal Binge Eating Cues

Imagine yourself walking into a movie theater. As you enter the lobby, you are surrounded by the sights and smells of the concession stand. Do you find yourself automatically starting to crave popcorn or your favorite candy? If you are someone who usually snacks at the movie theater, you might find yourself getting food and eating it on autopilot, without the sense of having made a conscious choice. This kind of automatic eating habit can make it difficult to stick to your eating plan and can set you up for binges.

Just like walking by one's regular pub can cause alcohol cravings in heavy drinkers, cues that are routinely associated with binge eating can trigger urges to binge. Binges often have a habitual element to them—they are associated with particular settings, foods, and thoughts. Our brains easily, and usually subconsciously, learn an association between the presence of certain cues in the environment and binge eating behavior (Jansen 1998). These cues can be foods that are a frequent part of your binge eating, or they can be more subtle elements of the environment, such as specific aromas, the bright lights of a fast-food restaurant, or even a certain time of day.

Activities or places that are a typical part of your binge, like stores where you tend to buy binge food, or even routes home from work past particular restaurants, may also be learned triggers for binge eating. Cues can also be internal; emotions, physical sensations, or thoughts that habitually precede a binge can put you into autopilot mode and lead to binges.

Think back to your most recent binge and try to identify the environmental cues that were present just before and during the binge:

	Just before binge	During binge
Place		
Activity		
Smells		
Sounds		
Physical sensations		
Sights		
Thoughts		
People		
Other		
Other		
Other		

Take a second now to review this list and circle any items that are a typical part of your binge routine.

Now that you've identified some typical cues, it's time to strategize how to change the patterns. The most effective strategy is to reduce your exposure to those cues—by getting rid of them, avoiding them, or replacing them with something less triggering. For example, you might change your route home to avoid walking past your favorite pizza place, particularly when you're feeling stressed. If the sensation of hunger is a trigger, revisit your meal plan to make sure that you're eating enough throughout the day and that you're not going too long between meals.

Some cues might not be totally avoidable, like negative interactions with your boss. For triggers that you can't entirely eliminate, develop a plan to cope in a different way. One strategy is to engage in a behavior that is incompatible with binge eating. For example, you might plan to meet a friend after a difficult day at work so that you're not home alone, or take a hot bath as a means of self-soothing in a way that would make it challenging to simultaneously eat.

Alternatively, you might choose to spend some time challenging unhelpful thoughts (chapter 6) or practicing mindfulness (chapter 8). You have lots of new tools in your toolbox, so think back to strategies you've learned that could help you cope with unavoidable triggers. Take a moment now to reflect on your top five triggers and how you will avoid or cope differently with them.

Trigger: _____

Plan: _____

_____

Trigger: _____

Plan: _____

_____

Trigger: _____

Plan: _____

_____

Trigger: _____

Plan: _____

_____

Trigger: _____

Plan: _____

_____

Example: *Trigger:* Getting hungry while walking around the grocery store.

Plan: Shop for my groceries online after I've eaten a full meal.

Food Cues

Subtle cues about food from your environment can also impact the chances that you'll overeat or binge eat, without you even being aware of them. We know from studies that food imagery can subconsciously increase eating. In one experiment (Harris, Bargh, and Brownell 2009), adults were brought into a lab to watch a television show, and about half of them had commercials for food interspersed into the show. The people who had seen the commercials ended up eating more food in a later part of the experiment than those who had not seen food advertising, even though they didn't report feeling any hungrier and were not consciously aware of the impact of the ads. The effects of the advertising weren't limited to the foods in the commercials; those people also ate more of snack foods that weren't in the ads. Of course, televisions aren't the only devices that expose you to food imagery. Similar effects have been observed when people eat in places with pictures of pizza (Hall et al. 2015).

Just being around food images can increase your likelihood of mindless eating. Studies that measured brain waves in women with BED found that people who binge eat have a particularly difficult time redirecting their attention away from pictures of high-calorie foods (Svaldi et al. 2010). If you're accustomed to eating in front of a screen, it's likely that these kinds of advertisements are working against you and increasing the chances that you'll lose control of your eating.

Do you tend to eat in restaurants that have pictures of food? Do you follow social media accounts that heavily feature food? Does your commute involve exposure to billboards or ads inside of the bus or train? Is your home full of cooking, travel, or lifestyle magazines that feature pictures of food?

List all the ways that you are regularly exposed to food imagery. Then brainstorm a plan for how to reduce that exposure:

Food image triggers	Coping plan

Example:

Pictures of menu items at the food court	Take my lunch to the park after I buy it

Food branding is another subtle but powerful trigger for overeating or binge eating. Imagine walking by your favorite brand of snack food in the grocery store. Does merely seeing the packaging create a little internal pull to buy that product? Branding can influence our habitual behaviors (Marteau et al. 2012), which is why companies invest so much in creating recognizable brands.

If you can't completely remove a triggering food from your environment, you might consider changing the packaging. For example, asking your spouse to move his or her cookies out of the bright blue packaging and into a plain brown bag would reduce the subconscious triggering you experience when you go into the cupboard.

Although reducing your exposure to food triggers is useful as you break the binge eating habit, you may find that there are triggers you can't avoid or don't want to avoid forever. Another effective strategy is breaking the association between those cues and binge eating by intentionally getting exposure to those cues at a time when you will not binge in response. For example, if the smell of the bakery at the mall is a trigger, invite a friend to go shopping with you.

As discussed in chapter 3, it can also be helpful to gradually expose yourself to foods that are associated with binge eating in a context that would limit your chance to binge—for example, buying and savoring a single doughnut before going in to a meeting. If you have a therapist, you might try eating triggering foods in session, so that you have a chance to talk through any urges that come up.

Body-Shaming Cues

Have you had the experience of someone making negative comments about your weight or shape? Or someone trying to shame you into changing your eating habits? As you have probably experienced, feeling ashamed about your body or your eating does not help break your binge eating patterns and may even make them worse. Unfortunately, stigmatizing messages associating weight with willpower, attractiveness, or intelligence are pervasive in today's world (Tomiyama 2014). Exposure to weight-based stigma can create biological and psychological stress and, ironically, lead to binge eating.

Research on weight stigma consistently shows that having a body-shaming experience leads to overeating. In one study, researchers had average-weight individuals put on a "fat suit" and walk around their college campus. The individuals in the suits reported experiencing rejection and weight stigma, and later ate a greater amount of snack foods and soda than individuals who did not wear the suit as they walked around campus (Incollingo Rodriguez, Heldreth, and Tomiyama 2016). Similarly, higher-weight women who were shown a video depicting negative weight-based stereotypes later ate three times as many calories as similar-weight women who saw a non-shaming video (Schvey, Puhl, and Brownell 2011). As discussed in chapter 6, anything that makes you feel bad about your body can kick off a cycle of shame, low mood, and overeating.

What can you do to limit the effects of this toxic attitude on your eating choices? One important step you can take is to reduce exposure to messages that are body-shaming or pro-diet. These messages are often disguised as being pro-health but actually focus on weight or shape instead of health. For example, do you follow social media accounts that promote diet plans? Unfollow any account that makes you feel bad or stirs up a desire to diet. What about magazines that have before-and-after photos or that shame celebrities for their weight and shape? Avoid media coverage that shames people for their bodies, even if it's not targeted directly at you.

Do you end up seeing ads for diet products as you watch TV or use the Internet? Use technological fixes like recording and fast-forwarding, or ad blockers built into your browser, to eliminate your exposure to these messages.

"A nutritionist is a wonderful thing, but be careful who you go to. Someone who limits what you can eat is not going to help you stop bingeing. At least it didn't for me." —Mia

If there are people in your life who persistently make you feel bad about your body, you might consider reducing your contact with them or setting a firm boundary about them no longer discussing your weight or shape.

Take a moment here to brainstorm sources of weight stigma that you can cut out of your life:

_____

_____

_____

_____

_____

_____

Of course, there may be some sources of weight stigma that you can't avoid. In those instances, you'll want to be prepared with the tools you learned in chapter 6 to respond to any negative thoughts about yourself that those experiences stir up.

Interpersonal Cues

Think back to recent experiences you've had eating with others. Did those meals help you stay on track or did they interfere with your plan to break the binge eating cycle? Eating with others can lead to over- or under-eating depending on the circumstances (Higgs and Thomas 2016). Because we use the eating behaviors of others as a subtle, sometimes unconscious, cue for our own food choices, it's possible to be unhelpfully influenced by the other people sitting at your table.

On one hand, you might have a group of friends who encourage overeating or who serve foods and drinks that are binge triggers for you. Alternatively, you might find that you end up restricting around certain dining companions because you're concerned about what they think about your food choices or your weight. As highlighted in chapter 3, that restriction mindset can set you up for a later binge, even if you eat a sufficient number of calories.

The solution is not to avoid social settings, as sharing a meal with good company is an important part of a healthy relationship with food. Instead, identify people who you know set off a pattern of eating too much or too little. Think of something you can say to them or to yourself to stay on track.

Person and typical reaction	What I can say to them	What I can say to myself

Example:

My friend Alicia. She wants to binge together.	"I'm working on stopping my binge eating, so let's plan a night together that doesn't revolve around food."	
My mother. I feel like I have to show her I'm "dieting."	"I appreciate your concern, but I'm working on my binge eating in a way that works for me."	"I don't have to impress her. I just have to do what I know is right."

"Changing my behaviors was the catalyst to recovery for me. Breaking my rituals was uncomfortable, but it allowed me 'normal' experiences that were more social than my private, isolated eating rituals. Sometimes even the social aspect of 'normal' eating made me uncomfortable, but it built my confidence that I could do it and be okay." —Samuel

Distractions

Have you ever had the experience of opening a bag of chips as you watched TV, only to look down and realize that the whole bag was suddenly eaten? Although many people habitually engage in some other activity when eating alone, there's good evidence that distraction can lead to mindless eating and even to binges.

Eating in front of a screen is a common risky habit. Studies have shown that people eat more when watching TV or listening to the radio, even when there are no mentions of or displays of food (Bellisle, Dalix, and Slama 2004). It's important to note that the people in these studies who ate more in front of the TV or radio did not describe themselves as hungrier prior to the meal or more satiated afterward, so their food intake was completely disconnected from their body's cues for food.

Another common distraction trap is eating at your desk while working or responding to emails. In experiments where people have to make food choices while doing tricky mental work, they're more likely to choose foods based on pleasure rather than health (Shiv and Fedorikhin 1999). When other things are on your mind, it's harder to pay attention to your goals and easy to make a decision you will later regret.

Although the thought of eating a meal without the presence of distractions might seem boring or unpleasant, there's actually a lot to think about as you start to truly pay attention to the process of eating. Try to notice your own physiological reactions to food. Where do you feel your hunger? What are the signals your body sends as you get satiated? Tune in to the taste, texture, and pleasure of the food you're eating. Does your reaction to the food change over the course of the meal? Make a commitment to try at least one distraction-free meal per day, preferably during the meal when you are most likely to encounter your binge-eating triggers.

Environments That Support Health

Just like our environment and habits can contribute to binge eating, they can also be designed in a way that helps you to meet your health goals. By structuring your world in the right way, you will reduce your reliance on willpower and increase the automaticity of new, healthy habits.

FOLLOWING YOUR FOOD PLAN

The single most important change you can implement to beat binge eating is making it easier to follow the non-diet food plan you developed in chapter 3. By now, you should have several weeks of experience to help you determine how well you're doing with eating regularly and flexibly without letting yourself get too hungry.

If you find that you're having difficulty sticking with your plan, restructuring your environment can help. The first and most vital step is to make the foods in your plan easy to access (Marteau et al. 2012). That might mean moving your fruit bowl to the center of your table and making sure that healthy snacks are stashed in places where you tend to get hungry, like your desk or car.

You also need to be realistic with yourself—the pile of produce that you bought is not going to be helpful unless you have the time, energy, and desire to cook it. Make sure that you have easy, appealing options available on days when you are too overwhelmed or tired to spend time preparing food. That might mean stocking up on healthy frozen foods or knowing where you can get prepared food without exposing yourself to binge triggers.

What are three steps you could take to make it easier to follow through on your non-diet eating plan?

1. _____

2. _____

3. _____

Increasing Exercise

Exercise is an effective way to strengthen the brain mechanisms that help you to exert control over your eating behavior in the face of binge triggers. Even a single episode of aerobic activity can lead to neural changes that reduce the risk of overeating in the presence of high-calorie snack foods (Hall 2016). In addition to these helpful brain changes, engaging in exercise can set you into a positive spiral of feel-good endorphins, increased self-esteem, and more motivation to stick to your healthy, non-binge intentions.

If you'd like to add more exercise into your life, either for your health generally or as a part of your plan to beat binge eating, structure your environment in a way that makes it as easy as possible to get going. Think of yourself as creating "triggers" that will set you on autopilot toward a new exercise routine. As much as you can, try to make exercise a habit by linking it with a particular day and time or activity. If you decide that you will always go for a walk on Friday during lunch, it will feel less like a decision or chore and more like a natural part of your routine. If working out with others feels comfortable to you, make a plan to meet a friend and exercise together. It's a lot harder to decide you're too tired if you have a friend waiting for you.

> *"I wanted to free myself from rules when it came to eating, not inflict more. But getting into a healthy routine that was regimented and based on a foundation of exercising was absolutely imperative. I started with baby steps. Now I work out at least an hour a day. It was tough for the first two months. But now I can't go without working out. Staying healthy has become exciting and fun. I listen to healthy podcasts, read books, keep my house in order. All this takes good fuel, and now I embrace fuel to thrive!"* —Oliver

Take a moment here to identify three changes to your environment or routine that would help you to exercise:

1. _____

2. _____

3. _____

Now that you've identified changes that would reduce your likelihood of bingeing and increase the chances that you'll stick with your eating plan, it's time to get to work removing binge triggers and setting up cues for more effective coping. What do you need to do to get those ideas off the page and into the world around you? Remember, if your environment isn't working with you, it's working against you. The easier you can make it to follow through on your intentions, the more effortless it will feel to break the bingeing cycle and replace it with healthy new habits.

CHAPTER 11

Week 8: Connect to Your Values

"A difficult time can be more readily endured if we retain the conviction that our existence holds a purpose—a cause to pursue, a person to love, a goal to achieve."

—John Maxwell

Throughout this book, we have been encouraging you to make choices built on the deepest, most authentic sense of yourself. Rather than listening to "should" thoughts or the wishes of others, you've been working toward figuring out what is meaningful to you and how to build a life that moves you in that direction. This chapter is going to help you formalize the relationship between your behaviors and your values. It's not enough to know what you don't want in your life, like binge eating. You also need to know what you want to invite into your life and how to make your binge-free life feel full. People who perceive their lives to have meaning are more likely to engage in healthy eating and exercise behaviors in the future (Brassai, Piko, and Steger 2015).

What Are Values?

Values are what you want your life to be about, what gives you a sense of meaning and purpose (Harris 2009). Values describe a particular *way* that you want to approach the various aspects of your life. They're not what you do, but how you do it. Values define the person you want to be in the world. For example, you might value contributing to your community through activism, relating lovingly to your spouse, being patient and accepting with your children, or being innovative and creative in your work.

When we take actions that are in line with our values, our life feels full, vital, and meaningful. Values are what enable us to withstand challenges in pursuit of a bigger vision for our lives. Values are also how we make decisions when there is no right answer. For example, imagine having a conflict with a friend. If your most important values are connection and forgiveness, you might work to resolve the conflict or let it go. If, on the other hand, your most important values are assertiveness and autonomy, you might choose to stand firm even if it means the conflict persists. Values give shape to our moment-to-moment choices, but they are bigger than any one action or outcome.

Take a moment to write down the first things that come to mind when you think of your values. For now, include whatever comes to mind; as you work through this chapter, you will clarify and refine your list.

_____

_____

_____

It's important to distinguish values from some things that are often mistaken for values:

- **Values are not the same as goals.** Think of goals as a destination and values as your direction over the journey of life (Harris 2009). If you can check something off as "done," it's a goal and not a value. For example, raising a certain amount of money in a fundraiser is a goal, but giving back to your community is a value. Getting married might be a goal, but being loving is a value that is never finished. The power of values is that they guide the quality of your actions rather than dictating that any particular thing happens. You can choose to live in line with your values every day, even if your goals are in the future. As discussed in chapter 5, it's best if your goals and values are aligned, but they are separate driving forces in your life.

- **Values are not emotions.** For example, "happiness" is not a value. Most of us wish for positive emotional states and try to avoid negative ones, but our emotions are not always under our control. Values, on the other hand, are freely chosen. And you can act consistently with them no matter how you feel inside. You can't choose to feel happy when you get negative news at work, but you can choose to behave in a way that reflects your value of persistence, for example.

- **Values are not "good" or "bad."** They just are. Everyone has their own set of values, and they're as particular as your preference for music. It's not right to like opera or wrong to like classic rock—your preferences are your own and may or may not be aligned with those of other people in your life. It's important to distinguish between your true values and your thoughts about what you *should* value or what other people might want you to value.

Now that you know some of the common mistakes people make in trying to identify their values, revisit what you wrote above and make any relevant changes:

_____

_____

_____

Why Values Are Important

As described in chapter 10, our behaviors are often a sort of "reflex" in response to our thoughts or certain environmental cues. If you have the thought *I should try to lose weight,* you might start restricting; if you drive past a favored fast-food spot, you might pull into the drive-through before you even realize you've made a choice. Using values as an anchor for choices presents a different path forward. Although distressing thoughts and behavioral impulses will still occur, you won't let those internal experiences automatically lead to the same old behaviors. You can pause, create a space for choice, and instead let your values guide your behavior.

Studies have shown that people who identify and connect with their values show enhanced self-control, as evidenced through an increased tolerance for physical pain, greater persistence through difficult and boring work, and improved ability to delay immediate gratification in the service of long-term gain (Schmeichel and Vohs 2009). Research suggests that acting on values rather than emotional impulse is one of the key skills that allows people with eating disorders to benefit from a specific kind of therapy called *acceptance and commitment therapy* (Juarascio et al. 2013).

Identifying Your Values

For many people, identifying values is difficult. It might be scary to think about what matters most to you for fear that you will come up short. Or you might find that you've been conforming to other people's values for so long that you're not sure how to tell what comes from others versus from yourself. You might be so stuck in the challenges of day-to-day life that you're not accustomed to taking this broader perspective on your life's meaning. If you're struggling to identify your values, this section will help you to get some clarity.

On the next page, you'll find a list of values. As you read through them, ask yourself the following questions:

If I had everything I needed in life, how would I behave?

What do I want to stand for?

What do I hold to be most important?

Circle any words that answer these questions. There's also space at the bottom of the list to write in values that aren't listed.

Courage	Authenticity	Harmony	Nurturance
Honesty	Acceptance	Independence	Dignity
Faith	Openness	Generosity	Helpfulness
Kindness	Flexibility	Integrity	Tradition
Adventure	Peacefulness	Compassion	Caring
Stability	Loyalty	Mindfulness	Service
Connection with others	Commitment	Dependability	Challenge
Curiosity	Humor	Responsibility	Tolerance
Connection with nature	Originality	Forgiveness	Industriousness
Creativity	Rationality	Intimacy	Cooperation
Gratitude	Mastery	Vulnerability	Loving
Excitement	Learning	Hope	Strength
Passion	Justice	Humility	Interdependence

_____   _____   _____   _____

How might you apply the values you selected in the different domains of your life? For example, you might want to relate to your family lovingly or do your job with integrity. For each domain below that is applicable to you, write a phrase that describes what you value in that part of your life. If one of the domains below is not applicable to you, skip it; or if it's something you'd like to eventually have in your life, think about what you would value if that aspect of your life were present. If you came up with a value that isn't on the values list, feel free to include it here, just make sure that you are describing a *quality* you bring to that domain, not a specific, achievable goal.

Family: _____

Romantic relationships: _____

Friendships: _____

Work and occupation: _____

Hobbies and leisure: _____

Physical health: _____

Spirituality: _____

Community: _____

Take a moment to select three values from the list above that feel most important to you. What is your reaction to identifying these values? Often, people experience intense emotion when connecting to their values. Those feelings might be inspiration and vitality. Other people experience sadness at the recognition of how far their life has drifted from their values. In addition, identifying and acting toward the things that matter most in life can also stir up feelings of vulnerability. Whatever comes up for you, just notice that reaction and allow it to be present.

Taking Steps in a Valued Direction

Now that you have a clearer sense of your values, it's time to figure out how to enact those values in your everyday life. If you think of your values as the direction of your life, *committed actions* are the steps you take in that direction (Luoma, Hayes, and Walser 2007). When we take actions that are in line with our values, our lives feel rich and meaningful. As less of your life is taken up by binge eating and the consequences of binge eating, what different choices do you want to make in your life? What do you want to do with your time? What do you want to do with your money? How do you want to relate to others?

As you reflect on your values, you may find that only large actions spring to mind. While it is wonderful to have big goals in your life aligned with your values, the true power of values is in the small, daily choices you make. For example, if you want to be a supportive parent, that might mean something really big, like helping your children pay for college. But it can also be embodied in small ways, like putting your phone down when your children are talking to you, offering hugs when a friend is hurtful to them, or leaving them a note of encouragement before a big test.

> *"I fought behavior changes on the grounds that I needed to change my thinking before I could change my disordered behaviors. But when my focus became more on the people and connections around me—the things in my life I valued—than on food, my behavior and thinking changed naturally."* —Samuel

Take a moment now to revisit each of the values that you defined earlier and identify at least one small, medium, and large action you could take that would be in line with that value.

Value	Small action	Medium action	Large action

Example:

Helping my community	Putting a quarter in an expired meter	Bringing soup to a sick friend	Volunteering at my church fundraiser

Managing Barriers to Valued Actions

Once you've been able to identify steps that would bring you closer to your values, the real challenge begins: actually implementing those actions in your life. Although values-aligned actions lead to an overall feeling of fulfillment in life, they can stir up anxiety, sadness, or worry in the moment. There may also be practical barriers with which you need to contend. Finally, we sometimes neglect to take values-aligned actions because it's easier to maintain the status quo. Following through on your good intentions will require some proactive planning, including making use of the tools that you've learned throughout this book.

Take a moment now to reflect on barriers that might come up as you begin to take the steps you generated above. Then, as a way of increasing your motivation and reconnecting with your intention, identify what you would lose in your life if you did not follow through on your values-aligned action. Finally, write down any strategies you can use to cope with the challenges you identified. Those tools can be strategies from an earlier chapter of this book, tactics that have been successful in helping you overcome past challenges, or healthy habits that will support you in following through on your plans.

Action	Possible barriers	What I'd lose	Tools to cope

Example:

Volunteering at a church fundraiser	Feeling tired Worries about being judged by other people on the committee	Connection to my community Spiritual boost	Make sure to get a good night's sleep Tell myself I only have to stay an hour if I'm too tired Fill out a Helpful Thoughts Worksheet

Applying Your Values to Food and Eating

How does binge eating fit into the values that you identified for yourself? Does the secrecy of binge eating fit with values in your relationships? Does binge eating fit into the way you want to care for your physical health, your leisure time, or your spiritual life?

Most people find that the more their lives are aligned with their deepest values, the less space there is for binge eating. Connecting with your deepest values can also help break the cycle of over-valuing weight and subsequent dieting. If you think about what you really want your life to be about, it's likely that weight and shape does not rise to the top of the list. Would you want your tombstone to list your weight? If not, refocus your energy on the things that you want to define you as a person.

Go back to the top three values you identified above. How would eating fit into each one? For example, if your top value is being a supportive romantic partner, how might you make choices around food and eating patterns that would support those values? The clues for how to answer that question are embedded in the particulars of your situation and what being a "supportive partner" means in this context.

If you have a partner who is, for example, trying to better control their blood sugar, you might choose to learn two new recipes this week for low-glycemic-index meals. If you know that shame around eating or a desire to hide binge eating gets in the way of spending time with your partner in the evenings, you can commit to eating meals together, even if it means risking the vulnerability of your partner seeing eating behaviors you would normally hide. Or you might simply work on turning your attention at shared meals away from your own internal fears about food and toward your partner, truly listening to what he or she is saying and savoring the time that you have together.

You might also identify values-consistent actions that you've been avoiding because of concerns related to weight or shape. Perhaps you've been avoiding eating with others because you fear judgment about your food choices. Or you might have put off dating or seeking out new friendships because of your feelings about your body. Use this opportunity to think about what choices you would make if you were living from your deepest values rather than making decisions based on fear, doubt, and self-judgment.

Top values	Related food and eating choices
#1	
#2	
#3	

You may find that your mind is telling you it's not possible to make these value-aligned food and eating choices unless you have fully stopped binge eating or until you lose weight. Notice those thoughts and use the tools you've learned to examine whether those thoughts are accurate, balanced, and complete. It's entirely possible to live in line with your values, regardless of your current weight, shape, or eating patterns.

Creating a Values Affirmation

The final step in preparing to stay the course toward your valued life direction is to create a *values affirmation*. People who engage in self-affirmation are more likely to identify a need to engage in better health behaviors (Harris and Napper 2005). Reflection on personal values can also protect against the harmful effects of stress. People who were prompted to engage in affirmation of their most important values before being put in a stressful situation showed a decreased release of cortisol, a stress hormone (Creswell et al. 2005). By affirming your values on a regular basis, you will find that it's easier to engage in the values-aligned behaviors you designed and to give up binge eating for good.

For each of the top three values you selected above, take a moment now to write *why* that value is important to you:

Value 1: _____

_____

_____

Value 2: _____

_____

_____

Value 3: _____

_____

_____

Find a place to keep this list where you can see it every day. You might put a copy beside your bathroom mirror, or take a picture and make it the background of your phone or computer. Revisit these values daily to help you remember why you want to take the values-aligned actions you selected. As you continue to build a life that matches your values, you will experience greater vitality, a deeper sense of purpose, and a healthier relationship with food and yourself.

CHAPTER 12

Build Your Individualized Binge Eating Prevention Plan

"Success is not final. Failure is not fatal. It is the courage to continue that counts."

—Winston Churchill

Congratulations! You've learned the most effective tools to stop compulsive, mindless, emotional, and binge eating. Now it's time to gather all the tools that work best for you. No one else is just like you, so your flexible, healthy relationship with food and your healthy coping tool kit will be unique. In this final chapter, you'll specify elements of your success and prepare to prevent relapse. Your final exercise will be to build your own binge eating prevention plan.

Be Proud of Yourself!

The past eight weeks have not been easy. Likely, they've been downright challenging. And likely you've had a couple binges take you momentarily off course. But that's to be expected. Don't be hard on yourself. In fact, let's take the time right now to acknowledge and commend all that you have learned so far.

By taking time to educate yourself, you got ready for change. You learned what binge eating is and what it is not.

- Binge eating is a pattern of loss of control with food.

- Binge eating causes distress.

- Binge eating has both biological and psychological causes.

- Binge eating is not only about food.

- Binge eating is a cycle—not a failure of willpower.

- Binge eating recovery is not hopeless.

You know that brain-based and genetic factors may have made you vulnerable, but binge eating is not your destiny. How has your thinking about binge eating changed?

_____

_____

_____

_____

You learned that creating a new-normal relationship with food is possible. You discovered that there are healthier responses to autopilot urges.

- Self-help can be as effective as in-person treatment.

- Binge eating can be overcome.

- The keys central to your recovery can be identified and understood.

- Your path to peace with food will be unique.

- No challenge, no change.

You learned the truth about diets. Armed with this information, you can make wise choices.

- The diet mindset can paradoxically contribute to binge eating.

- Messages about dieting are pervasive, but dieting is not an effective way to get healthy.

- Your odds of maintaining a significant weight loss after dieting are only slightly better than winning the lottery.

- If you have a history of dieting, stress may make you vulnerable to binge eating.

- Subtle diet messages may hide in your thoughts and behaviors.

- Your mind and body are wired to rebel against food deprivation.

- Regular non-diet eating is key to stopping binge eating.

- Healthy, normal eating is different for everyone.

Write your own definition of "normal eating."

_____

_____

_____

_____

You wrote your own sustainable, personalized eating plan. You adopted a radically different, health-oriented plan for eating.

Take a few minutes to evaluate how you've enacted your plan.

Have you given up dieting?	Yes	No
Are you planning well?	Yes	No
Are you eating every three to four hours?	Yes	No
Are you choosing foods you enjoy?	Yes	No
Are you including all food groups?	Yes	No
Are you making sure not to skip any meals or snacks?	Yes	No
Are you eating enough to be satisfied?	Yes	No
Are you following your plan?	Yes	No
Are you paying attention when you eat?	Yes	No

Reflect on what is working well in following your eating plan:

_____

_____

_____

_____

You practiced tools that are proven to reduce compulsive eating and increase peace with food. You've tried to:

- Visualize success.

- Expand optimism that your future is no longer marked by losing control with food.

- Set powerful, effective goals.

- Replace negative thinking patterns with accurate, balanced, and complete thoughts.

- Change food and body thoughts to be helpful.

- Label, accept, and face emotions without using food.

- Act intentionally, not based on cravings or urges.

- Write about difficult situations to manage emotions.

- Reach out to people, not food.

- Empower your healthy self, like you would your best friend.

- Cultivate positive emotions.

- Seek out soulful comforts.

- Pay attention purposely.

- Meditate to reduce reactivity.

- Eat for nutrition, pleasure, and energy.

- Tune in and respond to hunger and fullness cues.

- Heal, improve, and broaden relationships.

- Communicate effectively, honestly, and compassionately.

- Reduce environmental triggers.

- Create an environment that supports healthy eating and physical activity.

- Let your values guide sustainable change.

Which skills are the easiest for you?

_____

_____

_____

_____

Which skills are most challenging for you?

_____

_____

_____

_____

"Slowly there became this joy from the little changes I made. I'm talking little. But add up all the little changes day by day and they made big changes." —Isaiah

Though you have acquired all of these tools, success takes patience. If you haven't made as much progress as you hoped, or you find yourself struggling with lingering binge eating symptoms, don't give up. _Remember, full recovery from binge eating is possible—and it's possible for you!_ Plan how, where, and when you'll continue your journey. Start by answering the following questions:

Do you need more time with particular chapters and skills?   Yes   No

If so, which ones? _____

Could it be helpful to complete the whole workbook again?   Yes   No

If so, when will you begin? _____

Can you identify where you are most stuck?   Yes   No

If so, what will you change about how you use this workbook? _____

Would it be helpful to complete the workbook with a friend?   Yes   No

If so, who will you ask? _____

Do you believe that in-person professional help might be better for you?   Yes   No

If so, where will you seek out a professional? _____

When seeking resources, you'll need to be your own gatekeeper. Separate those that are offering evidence-based methods for healing your relationship with food from those offering short-term fixes, fads, and diets. If you are not making progress, we recommend you find a therapist, registered dietitian, or physician who specializes in eating disorders. Steer clear of deprivation-based eating and weight-focused programs.

Face Setbacks Early

It is helpful to prepare for problems as you plan for success. It is inevitable that you will stumble because difficult situations will arise. Some of those will be predictable, others may surprise you. How you respond is what makes all the difference in the long run. Every time you choose healthy actions, instead of habitual or mindless reactions, you strengthen your neural pathway to success. Let's look ahead to difficult situations on the horizon that may trigger you and the warning signs that may signal potential setbacks.

Anticipate Predictable Difficult Situations

What barriers to success can you anticipate being most challenging during the next three months? Some high-risk situations occur regularly, such as weekly stressful lunch meetings, a night of the week when you tend to feel lonely, or having to tackle an unpleasant task. Other barriers may happen once or occasionally, such as moving, asking for a raise, special events, travel, visitors, or a recurrence of anxiety or depression.

Consult your calendar to see what's ahead. Identify challenging situations you will face this month, next month, and the following month. Complete the chart below to be well prepared.

	Challenging situation I can anticipate	One time or recurring event?	Potential eating pitfalls	What would be more helpful?
This month				
Next month				
Third month				

Example:

	Challenging situations I can anticipate	One time or recurring event?	Potential eating pitfalls	What would be more helpful?
This month	Paying bills	Recurring	Mindlessly eat chips	Play favorite music to make it more pleasant
	Monday nights after bowling, drive home late and hungry	Recurring	Go on autopilot to a drive-through, order binge foods, eat while driving. Get home and feel disgusted.	Bring an enjoyable snack to eat at bowling. Get home feeling comfortably hungry. Make an easy meal, maybe a burrito.
Next month	Travel with friends	One time	Restrict at meals in front of friends, then secretly eat what I like in my hotel room	Give myself permission to choose foods I like and eat enough at meals
Third month	Attend a friend's birthday party	Recurring	Cancel plans, isolate, and binge eat	Attend to and focus on strengthening my relationships

Identify Warning Signs for Unexpected Problems

Mastery is achievable if you don't give up. Whether you are facing one of the predictable barriers you mentioned above or a slip, lapse, or relapse that sneaks up on you, keep in mind that you are on a journey.

- **A slip** is a small risky behavior. It does not lead to any binge eating problems because you return to effective coping from your tool kit.

- **A lapse** is a temporary stumble, a binge eating behavior that you regret. It motivates you to get back to effective coping from your tool kit.

- **A relapse** occurs when one mistake is followed by more. The behaviors lead away from effective coping and back to the binge eating cycle.

As you improve your coping skills and gain confidence, you'll get back on track faster after setbacks. It is important to identify warning signs that signal when you are struggling so you can intervene early. The process is similar to when you first learned to ride a bike. It will take some falls before you learn to spot all of the warning signs that precede losing control. Over time, the warning signs will cue you to make adjustments in your coping that lead you to stumble slightly rather than fall. Eventually, the warnings signs will lead to effective coping and you'll be able to stay on track.

What are your personal early warning signs of slips, lapses, and relapses? Identify helpful actions you can take in response.

Warning signs of a slip:	Actions to take:
Warning signs of a lapse:	Actions to take:
Warnings signs of a relapse:	Actions to take:

Example:

Warning signs of a slip:	Actions to take:
Letting myself get too hungry	Make and commit to a meal plan for the next several days, including three meals and three snacks.
Warning signs of a lapse:	Actions to take:
Emotional overeating, urge to binge eat in response	Fill out a Helpful Thoughts Worksheet when I feel tempted to binge eat after using food to soothe my emotions.
Warnings signs of a relapse:	Actions to take:
Return of the diet mentality	Reread chapter 4 and challenge my all-or-nothing thinking about food.

Building Your Personalized Binge Eating Prevention Plan

The information-gathering, skill-building, myth-busting portion of this workbook is complete. You have finished your own personal experiment during the past eight weeks! We hope the stories and quotes from those who have recovered have inspired you, and that the skills you practiced have challenged and changed you. You're ready to build your personalized Binge Eating Prevention Plan (BEPP). Each of the following will be a component:

- Start with the ABCs of Success

- Write out or revise the My Eating Plan worksheet

- Transform what you've learned into the My Go-To Tool Kit

- Build your personalized Wheel of Healthy Coping

BINGE EATING PREVENTION PLAN

ABCs of Success

Effective coping depends on having an easy-to-apply strategy. The ABCs of Success will enable you to choose intentional responses rather than default to impulsive reactions. In the space between a trigger and an action, there is a *choice point*. In difficult situations or when you notice a warning sign, pause and implement the ABCs of Success for relapse prevention.

Agree to "play the tape through."

It can be tempting to focus only on the favorable aspects of fantasies and impulsive thoughts, and to ignore the potential negative effects. Instead, pause and think realistically about the consequences of the actions you are considering. You'll make wiser decisions when you confront the fact that the fantasy is just one part of the story.

How do you do this? Pause and consider the bigger picture. For instance, let's say that you start fantasizing about skipping the workout class you signed up for to stay home alone and binge eat. Stop and notice the urge. Then ask yourself, *What happens when I play the tape through?* You might think, *I know I'll feel miserable if I stay home alone compulsively eating. I won't want to see my friends tonight because I'll be disgusted. I know I'll feel strong and satisfied if I work out. I know what I will get and give up depending on my choice.*

Reflect on a time when *playing the tape through* would have changed your actions and improved the outcome.

_____

_____

_____

_____

_____

_____

Believe you will do the next right thing.

This strategy can be invaluable when you're overly hungry or find yourself eating mindlessly. Small steps increase confidence, set you in a positive direction, and lead to big changes. Use your tool kit and eating plan to choose the next right thing.

As with the previous step, stop and notice the urge. For instance, let's say you just arrived at a drive-through that has been the start of a binge in the past. What is the next right thing to do? You might tell yourself, *I can park my car and meditate for ten minutes.*

Reflect on a time when *doing the next right thing* would have changed your actions and improved the outcome.

_____

_____

_____

_____

_____

_____

Commit to surfing the urge.

You know that urges, cravings, food obsessions, and triggers will occur even when you play the tape through and choose to do the next right thing. Accept their presence and wait for them to pass to strengthen your resilience. Thoughts and urges don't have to dictate your actions. As you know from the mindfulness chapter, urges come in cycles, similar to waves coming to shore. Use the practice of paying attention to your breath to ride out the urge until it dissipates. For instance, let's say that you are upset after a disagreement with your partner and want to soothe yourself with food. How can you commit to surfing the urge? Perhaps you tell yourself, *I'll set the timer on my phone for thirty minutes to show myself I can get through the urge without impulsively going to food. I will try a one- to two-minute meditation then take my dog for a walk to change my environment.*

Reflect on a time when *surfing the urge* would have changed your actions and improved the outcome.

_____

_____

_____

_____

_____

My Eating Plan

You've been practicing eating regularly, not dieting, and establishing your own guidelines. Based on your experience, schedule, preferences, and body's nutritional needs, make an updated eating plan each week. Download blank copies of this worksheet at http://www.newharbinger.com/43614.

My Eating Plan: Week # _____

The day(s) I will **shop** for the food I need this week:

_____

The day(s) I will **prepare** food for the week:

_____

The day I will **start** my new regular eating: _____

My non-diet eating guidelines are: _____

_____

_____

_____

_____

_____

_____

Weekdays

Meals & snacks	Time	Option 1	Option 2
Breakfast			
Snack			
Lunch			
Snack			
Dinner			
Snack			

Weekends

Meals & snacks	Time	Option 1	Option 2
Breakfast			
Snack			
Lunch			
Snack			
Dinner			
Snack			

My Go-To Tool Kit

Using the chart below, review each of the tools you've learned and practiced throughout this workbook. Think about the significance of each when it comes to your success. If you consider the tool important to your success each week, place a checkmark under "Weekly tools." If you consider the tool helpful but not necessary to implement weekly, place a checkmark under "As-needed tools." Be sure to include a checkmark for *every* item.

Tools in my tool kit	Weekly tools	As-needed tools
Visualizing		
Cultivate optimism about success.		
Read My Success Visualization script twice a day.		
Read My Process Visualization script daily.		
Update my visualization scripts.		
Goal-Setting		
Set specific, measurable goals.		
Make goals ambitious but reachable.		
Make goals short term and time limited.		
Remind myself why my goals matter.		
Set goals I want to move toward.		
Share my goals.		
Evaluate my progress.		
Thinking		
Identify thoughts that lead to difficulties.		
Challenge unhelpful thoughts.		
Fill out a Helpful Thoughts Worksheet.		

Tools in my tool kit	Weekly tools	As-needed tools
Change all-or-nothing and loss-of-control thinking about food.		
Start an activity when obsessing about food.		
Acknowledge and move past food thoughts.		
Reduce my emphasis on my body shape or size.		
Emotions		
Label my emotions.		
Accept that all emotions have a purpose.		
Use positive coping skills to handle distress.		
Write expressively.		
Reach out to people.		
Rely on facts.		
Take an opposite action.		
Empower my healthy self.		
Spend time in nature.		
Participate in a spiritual activity.		
Do something that brings me pleasure.		
Engage in an altruistic interest.		
Read uplifting statements.		
Utilize distractions.		
Accept that cravings and urges arise.		
Get adequate sleep to avoid emotion amplification.		

Tools in my tool kit	Weekly tools	As-needed tools
Harness choice points between emotions and actions.		
Ride out urges, cravings, and difficult emotions.		
Mindfulness		
Be present and pay attention on purpose.		
Cultivate a beginner's mind.		
Embrace nonjudgment with radical acceptance.		
Meditate for twenty minutes daily.		
Reduce multitasking and partial attention while eating.		
Take brief one- to two-minute meditation breaks.		
Experience the taste, pleasure, and quality of food.		
Pay attention to my nutritional needs.		
Eat in response to gentle hunger cues.		
Stop eating when comfortably full.		
Take a step back from cravings and urges.		
Relationships		
Increase closeness in important relationships.		
Adapt to a role change or transition.		
Re-engage after a loss.		
Expand the quantity of my relationships.		
Treat myself with kindness.		
Accept that being imperfect is being human.		

Tools in my tool kit	Weekly tools	As-needed tools
Communicate clearly and kindly.		
Listen to and validate others.		
De-escalate intense or unsafe situations.		
Choose wise resolutions that lead to more happiness.		
Environment		
Identify a personal binge eating cue.		
Plan a new strategy for one predictable environmental or interpersonal trigger.		
Reduce exposure to problematic food cues.		
Reduce exposure to body shaming triggers.		
Change my routine to increase exercise.		
Have at least one distraction-free meal per day.		
Values		
Revisit my list of values.		
Identify small, doable behaviors that align with my values.		
Try a new behavior to move closer to one of my values.		
Reread my values affirmation.		

Now it's time to build your Weekly Tool Kit. Using the checklist above, write down each of the tools you checked off in the "Weekly tools" column in the worksheet that follows (or download the worksheet from http://www.newharbinger.com/43614). Next to each tool, write down an action-oriented plan to put the tool to use. For example, *Success visualization: I'll read the script each morning before having coffee.*

My Weekly Tool Kit

For each skill category, write down the specific tool you find helpful on a weekly basis. Next to it, plan how you will implement the tool.

Visualizing tools _____

_____

_____

_____

_____

Goal-setting tools _____

_____

_____

_____

_____

Thinking tools _____

_____

_____

_____

_____

Emotion tools _____

_____

_____

_____

_____

_____

Mindfulness tools _____

_____

_____

_____

_____

_____

Relationship tools _____

_____

_____

_____

_____

_____

Environment tools _____

_____

_____

_____

_____

_____

Values tools _____

_____

_____

_____

_____

_____

Now that your Weekly Tool Kit is all set, fill out the summary component of your Binge Eating Prevention Plan, the Wheel of Healthy Coping, on the next page. It's a helpful way to visualize your BEPP and keep yourself on track. Write key words or phrases in each section that instantly remind you of your goals and how to attain them. Post the wheel where you will see it often as a quick reminder that you can do this!

Wheel of Healthy Coping

This exercise is designed to expand your effectiveness, enhance your relationships, and help you to live life more freely. In each slice of the pie, write keywords or phrases that instantly remind you of the tools you will practice to achieve your goals. Refer to your Weekly Tool Kit if you need help. And as your skills develop, you can update this chart by downloading blank copies from http://www.newharbinger.com/43614.

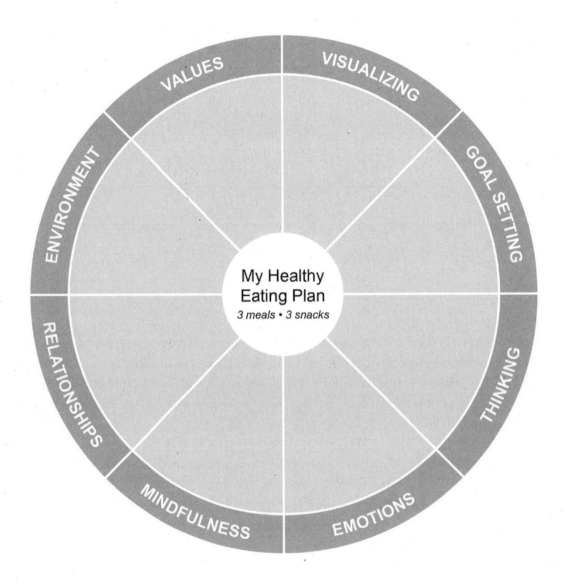

The next important step is to track your progress weekly and re-evaluate your plan. Choose the day you will review your progress and re-evaluate for success: _____.

Track your progress each week by marking every day that is free of binge eating. Once you have three consecutive months of freedom with food, re-evaluate monthly instead of weekly.

There are online apps for tracking goals, such as Coach.me, Strides, GoalsOnTrack, and Way of Life, to name just some. Or you can use a table as simple as the one below. No need to mark days you didn't reach your goal; focus on reinforcing your successes.

Monday	Tuesday	Wednesday	Thursday	Friday	Saturday	Sunday

Remember that every mistake you learn from today is an opportunity for success tomorrow. Journal about why you had this outcome.

_____

_____

_____

_____

_____

Review this week's eating plan. What about it worked well? What changes might help?

_____

_____

_____

_____

_____

Review your Weekly Tool Kit. Which tools were most helpful? Should you add from the as-needed tools list?

_____

_____

_____

_____

_____

Each week, using what you learn from reviewing your tracking, eating plan, and tool kit, build on your success by reevaluating and updating the core components of your BEPP (and keep them nearby for easy access):

My Eating Plan

Wheel of Healthy Coping

You've completed this workbook! We hope you offer yourself some gratitude for the time, energy, and strength you've chosen to invest in yourself. We are grateful to have been able to share these science-backed strategies, our clinical expertise, and the soulful lessons of people who have recovered. Whether you have reached mastery yet or not, you've taken meaningful steps on your path to peace with food. You're ready to transform how you eat, deal with stress, connect with people, and live the life you want!

Acknowledgments

Thank you to...

... Mike, for inspiring me with your humble brilliance and loving partnership.

Emma, for sharing your compassion, clarity, exquisite artistry and observations, and no space.

Gidget, for sharing your humor, advocacy, seemingly infinite curiosity and knowledge, and best days.

My mother, for your strength and love.

My father, for teaching me that sensitivity is a gift, and to meditate.

Tommy and Stacey, who make this world friendly.

All of my family for your support.

Carolyn Costin, for bringing the language of the soul into the science of healing.

My esteemed colleagues Drs. Rosen, Jakle, Corb, and Tracey Engleson, for generously contributing your expertise and wisdom.

Jennye, for your vision for our message. Caleb and Marisa, for your insightful editing.

Teachers, researchers, and clinicians who share what you know about well-being.

My clients, for your honest journeys and contagious courage.

And, to Danielle, for your kindness and your endless commitment to justice and excellence.

I am grateful.

—Gia

... To Gia, for being a wonderful teacher and friend. To my students at UCLA, for inspiring me to be a better therapist every day. To my clients, for letting me be a part of their journeys. To the supervisors at the UCLA Psychology Clinic, for their generosity and wisdom, and especially to Greg Serpa, for being the embodiment of insight and compassion. To Jennye, for helping to bring this project to life. To my parents and my extended family, for their unwavering support no matter the goal. And to my husband and my daughter, for being everything to me.

—Danielle

References

Adam, T. C., and E. S. Epel. 2007. "Stress, Eating, and the Reward System." *Physiological Behavior* 91: 449–458.

Adams, A. J. 2009. "Seeing Is Believing: The Power of Visualization." *Psychology Today* online. Dec. 3.

Allen, K. L., S. M. Byrne, M. La Puma, N. McLean, and E. A. Davis. 2008. "The Onset and Course of Binge Eating in 8- to 13-Year-Old Healthy Weight, Overweight and Obese Children." *Eating Behaviors* 9: 438–446.

American Psychiatric Association. 2013. *Diagnostic and Statistical Manual of Mental Disorders: DSM-5.* Arlington, VA: American Psychiatric Association.

Anton, N., E. Bean, S. Hammonds, and D. Stefanidis. 2017. "Application of Mental Skills Training in Surgery: A Review of Effectiveness and Proposed Next Steps." *Journal of Laparoendoscopic & Advanced Surgical Techniques* 27: 459–469.

Armatage, C. 2007. "Effects of an Implementation-Based Intervention on Fruit Consumption." *Psychology & Health* 22: 917–928.

Bacon, L., and A. Lucy. 2011. "Weight Science: Evaluating the Evidence for a Paradigm Shift." *Nutrition Journal* 10. https://doi.org/10.1186/1475-2891-10-9.

Balodis, I. M., H. Kober, P. D. Worhunsky, M. A. White, M. C. Stevens, G. D. Pearlson, R. Sinha, C. M. Grilo, and M. N. Potenza. 2013. "Monetary Reward Processing in Obese Individuals with and Without Binge Eating Disorder." *Biological Psychiatry* 73: 877–886.

Barlow, D., K. Ellard, C. Fairholme, T. Farchione, C. Boisseau, L. Allen, and J. Ehrenreich-May. 2011. *Unified Protocol for Transdiagnostic Treatment of Emotional Disorders.* New York: Oxford University Press.

Beck, J. S. 2011. *Cognitive Behavior Therapy: Basics and Beyond.* 2nd ed. New York: Guilford Press.

Bellisle, F., A. M. Dalix, and G. Slama. 2004. "Non Food-Related Environmental Stimuli Induce Increased Meal Intake in Healthy Women: Comparison of Television Viewing versus Listening to a Recorded Story in Laboratory Settings." *Appetite* 43: 175–180.

Bieler, D. 2016. "Penn State Kicker Joey Julius Opens Up About Struggles with Binge Eating Disorder." *The Washington Post,* October 3.

Blomquist, K. K., E. B. Ansell, M. A. White, R. M. Masheb, and C. M. Grilo. 2012. "Interpersonal Problems and Developmental Trajectories of Binge Eating Disorder." *Comprehensive Psychiatry* 53: 1,088–1,095.

Boggiano, M., J. Dorsey, J. Thomas, and D. Murdaugh. 2009. "The Pavlovian Power of Palatable Food: Lessons for Weight-Loss Adherence from a New Rodent Model of Cue-Induced Overeating." *International Journal of Obesity* 33: 693–701.

Boggiano, P. C., J. B. Chandler, K. D. Viana, C. R. Oswald, and P. K. Wauford. 2005. "Combined Dieting and Stress Evoke Exaggerated Responses to Opioids in Binge Eating Rats." *Behavioral Neuroscience* 119: 1,207–1,214.

Bowen, S., and A. Marlatt. 2009. "Surfing the Urge: Brief Mindfulness-Based Intervention for College student Smokers." *Psychology of Addictive Behaviors* 23: 666–671.

Bowler, D., L. M. Buyung-Ali, T. M. Knight, and A. S. Pullin. 2010. "A Systematic Review of Evidence for the Added Benefits to Health of Exposure to Natural Environments." *BMC Public Health* 10: 456.

Bowman, B. 2016. *The Golden Rules.* New York: St. Martin's Press.

Brach, T. 2003. *Radical Acceptance.* New York: Bantam Books.

Brassai, L., B. F. Piko, and M. F. Steger. 2015. "A Reason to Stay Healthy: The Role of Meaning in Life in Relation to Physical Activity and Healthy Eating Among Adolescents." *Journal of Health Psychology* 20: 473–482.

Brown, B. 2010. *The Gifts of Imperfection: Let Go of Who You Think You're Supposed to Be and Embrace Who You Are.* Center City, Minnesota: Hazelden Publishing.

Burns, D. 2008. *Feeling Good Together: The Secret to Making Troubled Relationships Work.* New York: Broadway Books.

Callow, N., R. Roberts, L. Hardy, D. Jiang, and M. G. Edwards. 2013. "Performance Improvements from Imagery: Evidence That Internal Visual Imagery Is Superior to External Visual Imagery for Slalom Performance." *Frontiers in Human Neuroscience* 7: 697.

Carter, J. C., and C. G. Fairburn. 1998. "Cognitive-Behavioral Self-Help for Binge Eating Disorder: A Controlled Effectiveness Study." *Journal of Consulting and Clinical Psychology* 66: 616–623.

Chun, M. H., M. C. Chang, and S.-J. Lee. 2017. "The Effects of Forest Therapy on Depression and Anxiety in Patients with Chronic Stroke." *International Journal of Neuroscience* 127: 199–203.

Clarey, C. 2014. "Olympians Use Imagery as Mental Training." *The New York Times.* February 22.

Cocks, M., C.-A. Moulton, S. Luu, and T. Cil. 2014. "What Surgeons Can Learn from Athletes: Mental Practice in Sports and Surgery." *Journal of Surgical Education* 71: 262–269.

Conversano, C., A. Rotondo, E. Lensi, O. D. Vista, F. Arpone, and M. A. Reda. 2010. "Optimism and Its Impact on Mental and Physical Well Being." *Clinical Practice and Epidemiology in Mental Health* 6: 25–29.

Cooper, M., G. Todd, and H. Turner. 2007. "The Effects of Using Imagery to Modify Core Emotional Beliefs in Bulimia Nervosa: An Experimental Pilot Study." *Journal of Cognitive Psychotherapy* 21: 117–122.

Corstophine, E. 2006. "Cognitive-Emotional-Behavioral Therapy for Eating Disorders: Working with Beliefs About Emotions." *European Eating Disorders Review* 14: 448–461.

Costin, C., and G. Grabb. 2011. *8 Keys to Recovery from an Eating Disorder: Effective Strategies from Therapeutic Practice and Personal Experience.* New York: W.W. Norton.

Creswell, J. D., W. T. Welch, S. E. Taylor, D. K. Sherman, T. L. Gruenewald, and T. Mann. 2005. "Affirmation of Personal Values Buffers Neuroendocrine and Psychological Stress Responses." *Psychological Science* 16: 846–851.

Dakanalis, A., M. Clerici, M. Caslini, S. Gaudio, S. Serino, G. Riva, and G. Carrà. 2016. "Predictors of Initiation and Persistence of Recurrent Binge Eating and Inappropriate Weight Compensatory Behaviors in College Men." *International Journal of Eating Disorders* 49: 581–590.

Day, T., and P. Tosey. 2011. "Beyond SMART? A New Framework for Goal Setting." *Curriculum Journal* 22: 515–534.

Dingemans, A., U. Danner, and M. Parks. 2017. "Emotion Regulation in Binge Eating Disorder: A Review." *Nutrients* 9: 1,274.

Doran, G. T. 1981. "There's a S.M.A.R.T Way to Write Management's Goals and Objectives." *Management Review* 70: 35–36.

Dugmore, J. A., C. G. Winten, H. E. Niven, and J. Bauer. 2019. "Effects of Weight-Neutral Approaches Compared with Traditional Weight Loss Approaches on Behavioral, Physical, and Psychological Health Outcomes: A Systematic Review and Meta-Analysis." *Nutrition Reviews,* nuz020.

Dugue, R., F. Renner, M. Austermann, B. Tuschen-Caffier, and G. Jacob. 2018. "Imagery Rescripting in Individuals with Binge-Eating Behavior: An Experimental Proof-of-Concept Study." *International Journal of Eating Disorders* 52: 183–188.

Fairburn, C. 2013. *Overcoming Binge Eating.* New York: Guilford Press.

Fairburn, C. G. 2008. *Cognitive Behavior Therapy and Eating Disorders.* New York: Guilford Press.

Fairburn, C., G. Cooper, Z. & Shafran, R. (2003). Cognitive Behaviour Therapy for Eating Disorders: A "transdiagnostic" Theory and Treatment. *Behaviour Research and Therapy* 41, 509–528.

Fairburn, C. G., H. A. Doll, S. L. Welch, P. J. Hay, B. A. Davies, and M. E. O'Connor. 1998. "Risk Factors for Binge Eating Disorder." *Archives of General Psychiatry* 55: 425–432.

Fildes, A., J. Charlton, C. Rudisill, P. Littlejohns, A. T. Prevost, and M. Gulliford. 2015. "Probability of an Obese Person Attaining Normal Body Weight: Cohort Study Using Electronic Health Records." *American Journal of Public Health* 105: 54–59.

Filgueiras, A., E. F. Quintas Conde, and C. R. Hall. 2018. "The Neural Basis of Kinesthetic and Visual Imagery in Sports: An ALE Meta-Analysis." *Brain Imaging and Behavior* 12: 1,513.

Forman, E., K. L. Hoffman, K. B. McGrath, J. D. Herbert, L. L. Brandsma, and M. R. Lowe. 2007. "A Comparison of Acceptance and Control-Based Strategies for Coping with Food Cravings: An Analog Study." *Behavior Research and Therapy* 45: 2,372–2,386.

Fothergill, E., J. Guo, L. Howard, J. C. Kerns, N. D. Knuth, R. Brychta, K. Y. Chen, et al. 2016. "Persistent Metabolic Adaptation 6 Years after 'The Biggest Loser' Competition." *Obesity* 24: 1,612–1,619.

Frank, E., and J. Levenson. 2011. *Interpersonal Psychotherapy.* Washington, D.C.: American Psychological Association.

Franklin, J. C., and B. C. Scheile. 1948. "Observations on Human Behavior in Experimental Semi-Starvation and Rehabilitation." *Journal of Clinical Psychology* 4: 28–45.

Frattaroli, J. 2006. Experimental Disclosure and Its Moderators: A Meta-Analysis." *Psychological Bulletin* 132: 823–865.

French, S. A., R. W. Jeffery, J. L. Forster, P. G. McGovern, S. H. Kelder, and J. E. Baxter. 1994. "Predictors of Weight Change over Two Years Among a Population of Working Adults: The Healthy Worker Project." *International Journal of Obesity Related Metabolic Disorders* 18: 145–154.

Galla, B. M., G. A. O'Reilly, M. J. Kitil, S. L. Smalley, and D. S. Black. 2015. "Community-Based Mindfulness Program for Disease Prevention and Health Promotion: Targeting Stress Reduction." *American Journal of Health Promotion* 30: 36–41.

Gearhardt, A. N., C. Davis, R. Kuschner, and K. D. Brownell. 2011. "The Addiction Potential of Hyperpalatable Foods." *Current Drug Abuse Reviews* 4: 140–145.

Glasofer, D. R., D. A. F. Haaga, L. Hannallah, S. E. Field, M. Kozlosky, J. Reynolds, J. A. Yanovski, and M. Tanofsky-Kraff. 2013. "Self-Efficacy Beliefs and Eating Behavior in Adolescent Girls at-Risk for Excess Weight Gain and Binge Eating Disorder." *The International Journal of Eating Disorders* 46: 663–668.

Gluck, M. E., E. Yahav, S. A. Hashim, and A. Geliebter. 2014. "Ghrelin Levels after a Cold Pressor Stress Test in Obese Women with Binge Eating Disorder." *Psychosomatic Medicine* 76: 74–79.

Goyal, M., S. Singh, E. M. Sibinga, N. F. Gould, A. Rowland-Seymour, R. Sharma, Z. Berger, D. Sleicher, D. Maron, H. Shihab, et al. 2014. "Meditation Programs for Psychological Stress and Well-Being: A Systematic Review and Meta-Analysis." *JAMA Internal Medicine* 174: 357–368.

Grilo, C. M. 2013. "Why No Cognitive Body Image Feature such as Overvaluation of Shape/Weight in the Binge Eating Disorder Diagnosis?" *International Journal of Eating Disorders* 46: 208–211.

Grilo, C. M., M. A. White, R. Gueorguieva, G. T. Wilson, and R. M. Masheb. 2013. "Predictive Significance of the Overvaluation of Shape/Weight in Obese Patients with Binge Eating Disorder: Findings from a Randomized Controlled Trial with 12-Month Follow-Up." *Psychological Medicine* 43: 1,335–1,344.

Grilo, C. M., M. A. White, and R. M. Masheb. 2009. "DSM-IV Psychiatric Disorder Comorbidity and Its Correlates in Binge Eating Disorder." *International Journal of Eating Disorders* 42: 228–234.

Haedt-Matt, A. A., P. K Keel, S. E. Racine, S. A. Burt, J. Y. Hu, S. Boker, M. Neale, and K. L. Klump. 2014. "Do Emotional Eating Urges Regulate Affect? Concurrent and Prospective Associations and Implications for Risk Models of Binge Eating." *International Journal of Eating Disorders* 47: 874–877.

Hagan, M. M., and D. E. Moss. 1997. "Persistence of Binge-Eating Patterns after a History of Restriction with Intermittent Bouts of Refeeding on Palatable Foods in Rats: Implications for Bulimia Nervosa." *International Journal of Eating Disorders* 22: 411–420.

Hagan, M. M., P. K. Wauford, P. C. Chandler, L. A. Jarrett, R. J. Rybak, and K. Blackburn. 2002. "A New Animal Model of Binge Eating: Key Synergistic Role of Past Caloric Restriction and Stress." *Physiology & Behavior* 77: 45–54.

Hall, P. A. 2016. "Executive-Control Processes in High-Calorie Food Consumption." *Current Directions in Psychological Science* 25: 91–98.

Hall, P., B. Tran, C. Lowe, C. Vincent, M. Mourtzakis, T. Liu-Ambrose, H. Prapavessis, and Y. Gidron. 2015. "Expression of Executive Control in Situational Context: Effects of Facilitating versus Restraining Cues on Snack Food Consumption." *Health Psychology* 34: 539–546.

Hamilton, Lara. 2015. "*What is the Plate Method?*" American Diabetes Association. http://www.diabetes-forecast.org/2015/adm/diabetes-plate-method/what-is-the-plate-method.html (accessed May 1, 2018).

Harris, J. L., J. A. Bargh, and . D. Brownell. 2009. "Priming Effects of Television Food Advertising on Eating Behavior." *Health Psychology* 28: 404–413.

Harris, P. R., and L. Napper. 2005. "Self-Affirmation and the Biased Processing of Threatening Health-Risk Information." *Personality & Social Psychology Bulletin* 31: 1,250–1,263.

Harris, R.. 2009. *ACT Made Simple.* Oakland, CA: New Harbinger.

Hatter, A., M. Hagger, and S. Pal. 2015. "Weight-Loss Intervention Using Implementation Intentions and Mental Imagery: A Randomised Control Study Protocol." *BMC Public Health* 15: 196.

Higgs, S., and J. Thomas. 2016. "Social Influences on Eating." *Current Opinion in Behavioral Sciences* 9: 1–6.

Hilbert, A., and B. Tuschen-Caffier. 2005. "Body-Related Cognitions in Binge-Eating Disorder and Bulimia Nervosa." *Journal of Social and Clinical Psychology* 24: 561–579.

Hilton, L., S. Hempel, B. A. Ewing, E. Apaydin, L. Xenakis, S. Newberry, B. Colaiaco, A. R. Maher, R. M. Shanman, M. E. Sorbero, et al. 2017. "Mindfulness Meditation for Chronic Pain: A Systematic Review and Meta-Analysis." *Annals of Behavioral Medicine* 51: 199–213.

Hollenbeck, J. R., C. R. Williams, and H. J. Klein, H. J. 1989. "An Empirical Examination of the Antecedents of Commitment to Difficult Goals." *Journal of Applied Psychology* 74: 18–23.

Hudson, J. I., E. Hiripi, H. G. Pope Jr., and R. C. Kessler. 2007. "The Prevalence and Correlates of Eating Disorders in the National Comorbidity Survey Replication." *Biological Psychiatry* 61: 348–358.

Incollingo Rodriguez, A. C., C. M. Heldreth, and A. J. Tomiyama. 2016. "Putting on Weight Stigma: A Randomized Study of the Effects of Wearing a Fat Suit on Eating, Well-Being, and Cortisol." *Obesity* 24: 1,892–1,898.

Ivanova, I. V., G. A. Tasca, N. Hammond, L. Balfour, K. Ritchie, D. Koszycki, and H. Bissada. 2015. "Negative Affect Mediates the Relationship Between Interpersonal Problems and Binge-Eating Disorder Symptoms and Psychopathology in a Clinical Sample: A Test of the Interpersonal Model." *European Eating Disorders Review* 23: 133–138.

Jansen, A. 1998. "A Learning Model of Binge Eating: Cue Reactivity and Cue Exposure." *Behaviour Research and Therapy* 36: 257–272.

Jones, A. C., and N. R. Herr. 2018. "Emotion Differentiation Mediates the Association Between Emotion Regulation Difficulties and Caloric Intake." *Eating Behavior* 29: 35–40.

Juarascio, A., J. Shaw, E. Forman, C. A. Timko, J. Herbert, M. Butryn, D. Bunnell, A. Matteucci, and M. Lowe. 2013. "Acceptance and Commitment Therapy as a Novel Treatment for Eating Disorders: An Initial Test of Efficacy and Mediation." *Behavior Modification* 37: 459–489.

Kabat-Zinn, Jon (2012, 2016). Mindfulness for Beginners. Sounds True, Inc., Boulder, CO.

Kabat-Zinn, J. 2018. *Meditation Is Not What You Think: Mindfulness and Why It Is So Important.* New York: Hachette Books.

Katterman, S. N., B. M. Kleinman, M. M. Hood, L. M. Nackers, and J. A. Corsica. 2014. "Mindfulness Meditation as an Intervention for Binge Eating, Emotional Eating, and Weight Loss: A Systematic review." *Eating Behaviors* April 15(2): 197–204.

Kenardy, J., B. Arnow, and W. S. Agras. 1996. "The Aversiveness of Specific Emotional States Associated with Binge-Eating in Obese Subjects." *Australian and New Zealand Journal of Psychiatry* 30: 839–844.

Kendig, M. D., A. M. K. Cheung, J. S. Raymond, and L. H. Corbit. 2016. "Contexts Paired with Junk Food Impair Goal-Directed Behavior in Rats: Implications for Decision Making in Obesogenic Environments." *Frontiers in Behavioral Neuroscience* 10: 216.

Kelly, J., and J. D. Yeterian. 2012. "Empirical Awakening: The New Science on Mutual Help and Implications for Cost Containment Under Healthcare Reform." *Substance Abuse* 33: 85–89.

Kenny, T. E., C. Singleton, and J. C. Carter. 2017. "Testing Predictions of the Emotion Regulation Model of Binge-Eating Disorder." International Journal of Eating Disorders 50: 1297–1305. Kobayashi, H., S. Chorong, I. Harumi, P. Bum-Jin, L. Juyoung, K. Takahide, and M. Yoshifumi (2018). "Forest Walking Affects Autonomic Nervous Activity: A Population-Based Study." *Frontiers in Public Health* 6: 278.

Kircanski, K., M. D. Lieberman, and M. G. Craske. 2012. "Feelings into Words: Contributions of Language to Exposure Therapy." *Psychological Science* 23: 1,086–1,091.

Klump, K. L., K. M. Culbert, S. O'Connor, N. Fowler, and S. A. Burt. 2017. "The Significant Effects of Puberty on the Genetic Diathesis of Binge Eating in Girls." *International Journal of Eating Disorders* 50: 984–989.

Knauper, B., A. McCollam, A. Rosen-Brown, J. Lacaille, E. Kelso, and M. Roseman. 2011. "Fruitful Plans: Adding Targeted Mental Imagery to Implementation Intentions Increases Fruit Consumption." *Psychology and Health* 26: 601–617.

Kobayashi H, Song C, Ikei H, Park B-J, Lee J, Kagawa T and Miyazaki Y (2018) Forest Walking Affects Autonomic Nervous Activity: A Population-Based Study. *Frontiers in Public Health* 6:278. doi: 10.3389/fpubh.2018.00278

Kober, H., and R. G. Boswell. 2018. "Potential Psychological & Neural Mechanisms in Binge Eating Disorder: Implications for Treatment." *Clinical Psychology Review* 60: 32–44.

Kristeller, J., and A. Bowman. 2015. *The Joy of Half a Cookie*. London: Orion Publishing.

Kristeller, J., and C. B. Hallett. 1999. "An Exploratory Study of Meditation-Based Intervention for Binge Eating Disorder." *Journal of Health Psychology* 4: 357–363.

Kristeller, J., and R. Wolever. 2014. "Mindfulness-Based Eating Awareness Training: Treatment of Overeating and Obesity." In *Mindfulness Approaches*, 2nd ed., edited by R. A. Baer. San Diego, CA: Elsevier.

Kristeller, J., R. Q. Wolever, and V. Sheets. 2014. "Mindfulness-Based Eating Awareness Training (MB-EAT) for Binge Eating: A Randomized Clinical Trial." *Mindfulness* 5: 282–297.

Latham, G. P., and E. A. Locke. 1991. Self-Regulation Through Goal Setting. *Organizational Behavior and Human Decision Making* 50: 212-247.

Latham, G. P., and E. A. Locke. 2007. New Developments in and Directions for Goal Setting Research." *European Psychologist* 12: 290–300.

Leehr, E. J., K. Krohmer, K. Schag, T. Dresler, S. Zipfel, and K. E. Giel. 2015. "Emotion Regulation Model in Binge Eating Disorder and Obesity: A Systematic Review." *Neuroscience and Biobehavioral Reviews* 49: 125–134.

Lieberman, M. D., N. I. Eisenberger, M. J. Crockett, S. M. Tom, J. H. Pfeifer, and B. M. Way. 2007. "Putting Feelings into Words: Affect Labeling Disrupts Amygdala Activity to Affective Stimuli." *Psychological Science* 18: 421–428.

Lieberman, M. D., T. K. Inagaki, G. Tabibnia, and M. J. Crockett 2011. "Subjective Responses to Emotional Stimuli During Labeling, Reappraisal, and Distraction." *Emotion* 11: 468–480.

Lin, J., N. Chadi, and L. Shrier. 2019. "Mindfulness-Based Interventions for Adolescents. *Current Opinion Pediatrics* 31: 469–475.

Linehan, Marsha 1993. *Skills Training Manual for Treating Borderline Personality Disorder.* New York: Guilford Press.

Lingswiler, V. M., and J. H. Crowther. 1989. "Affective and Cognitive Antecedents to Eating Episodes in Bulimia and Binge Eating." *International Journal of Eating Disorders* 8: 533–539.

Locke, E. A. 1996. "Motivation Through Conscious Goal Setting." *Applied & Preventive Psychology* 5: 117–124.

Locke, E. A., and G. P. Latham. 2006. "New Directions in Goal-Setting Theory." *Current Directions in Psychological Science* 15: 265–268.

Luoma, J. B., S. C. Hayes, and R. D. Walser. 2007. *Learning ACT: An Acceptance & Commitment Therapy Skills-Training Manual for Therapists.* Oakland, CA: New Harbinger Publications.

Mann, T. 2015. *Secrets from the Eating Lab.* New York: Harper Collins.

Mann T., A. J. Tomiyama, E. Westling, A. M. Lew, B. Samuels, and J. Chatman. 2007. "Medicare's Search for Effective Obesity Treatments: Diets Are Not the Answer." *American Psychologist* 62: 220–233.

Marteau, T. M., G. J. Hollands, and P. C. Fletcher. 2012. "Changing Human Behavior to Prevent Disease: The Importance of Targeting Automatic Processes." *Science* 337: 1,492–1,495.

Masheb, R. M., C. M. Grilo, and M. A. White. 2011. "An Examination of Eating Patterns in Community Women with Bulimia Nervosa and Binge Eating Disorder." *International Journal of Eating Disorders* 44: 618–624.

Mason, T. B., and R. J. Lewis. 2015. "Assessing the Roles of Impulsivity, Food-Related Cognitions, BMI, and Demographics in the Dual Pathway Model of Binge Eating Among Men and Women." *Eating Behaviors* 18: 151–55.

Mathes, W. F., K. A. Brownley, X. Mo, and C. M. Bulik. 2009. "The Biology of Binge Eating." *Appetite* 52: 545–553.

McKay, M., J. Wood, and J. Brantley. 2007. *The Dialectical Behavior Therapy Skills Workbook: Practical DBT Exercises for Learning Mindfulness, Interpersonal Effectiveness, Emotion Regulation & Distress Tolerance.* Oakland, CA: New Harbinger Publications.

Miranda, J., S. Woo, I. Lagomasino, K. A. Hepner, S. Wiseman, and R. Munoz. 2006. *Group Cognitive Behavioral Therapy for Depression: Thoughts and Your Mood.* Cognitive Behavioral Depression Clinic,

Division of Psychosocial Medicine San Francisco General Hospital, University of California, San Francisco.

Miranda, R., M. Weierich, V. Khaita, J. Jurska, and S. Andersen. 2017. "Induced Optimism as Mental Rehearsal to Decrease Depressive Certainty." *Behavior Research and Therapy* 90: 1–8.

Mitchell, K. S., M. C. Neale, C. M. Bulik, S. H. Aggen, K. S. Kendler, and S. E. Mazzeo. 2010. "Binge Eating Disorder: A Symptom-Level Investigation of Genetic and Environmental Influences on Liability." *Psychological Medicine* 40: 1,899–1,906.

Monsel, S. 2003. "Task Switching." *Trends in Cognitive Science* 7: 134–140.

Monteleone, P., A. Tortorella, E. Castaldo, C. Di Filippo, and M. Maj. 2007. "The Leu72Met Polymorphism of the Ghrelin Gene Is Significantly Associated with Binge Eating Disorder." *Psychiatric Genetics* 17: 13–16.

Murphy, R., S. Straebler, S. Basden, Z. Cooper, and C. G. Fairburn. 2012. "Interpersonal Psychotherapy for Eating Disorders." *Clinical Psychology & Psychotherapy* 19: 150–158.

Neff, Kristin. 2020. *What is Self-Compassion?* Self-compassion.org. http://self-compassion.org/the-three-elements-of-self-compassion-2/ (accessed on January 10, 2020).

Neff, K., and C. Germer. 2018. *The Mindfulness Compassion Workbook: A Proven Way to Accept Yourself, Build Inner Strength and Thrive.* New York: Guilford Press.

Omichinski, L. 1996. *You Count, Calories Don't.* London: Hodder & Stoughton.

Pearson, C. M., D. S. Chester, D. Powell, S. A. Wonderlich, and G. T. Smith. 2016. "Investigating the Reinforcing Value of Binge Anticipation." *International Journal of Eating Disorders* 49: 539–541.

Pietiläinen, K. H., S. E. Saarni, J. Kaprio, and A. Rissanen. 2012. "Does Dieting Make You Fat? A Twin Study." *International Journal of Obesity* 36: 456–464.

Pink, D. 2009. *Drive.* New York: Riverhead Books.

Polivy, J., S. B. Zeitlin, C. P. Herman, and A. L. Beal. 1994. "Food Restriction and Binge Eating: A Study of Former Prisoners of War." *Journal of Abnormal Psychology* 103: 409–411.

Razzoli, M., C. Pearson, S. Crow, and A. Bartolomucci. 2017. "Stress, Overeating, and Obesity: Insights from Human Studies and Preclinical Models." *Neuroscience and Biobehavioral Reviews* 76: 154–162.

Rozin, P., and E. Rozyman. 2001. "Negativity Bias, Negativity Dominance, and Contagion." *Personality and Social Psychology Review* 5: 296–320.

Schag, K., J. Schönleber, M. Teufel, S. Zipfel, and K. E. Giel. 2013. "Food-Related Impulsivity in Obesity and Binge Eating Disorder: A Systematic Review." *Obesity Reviews* 14: 477–495.

Schmeichel, B. J., and K. Vohs. 2009. "Self-Affirmation and Self-Control: Affirming Core Values Counteracts Ego Depletion." *Journal of Personality and Social Psychology* 96: 770–782.

Schvey, N. A., R. M. Puhl, and K. D. Brownell. 2011. "The Impact of Weight Stigma on Caloric Consumption." *Obesity* 19: 1,957–1,962.

Seligman, M. 2002. *Authentic Happiness.* New York: Free Press.

Shiv, B., and A. Fedorikhin. 1999. "Heart and Mind in Conflict: The Interplay of Affect and Cognition in Consumer Decision Making." *Journal of Consumer Research* 26: 278–292.

Sifferlin, A. 2017. "The Weight Loss Trap: Why Your Diet Isn't Working." *Time*, May 25. Accessed July 4, 2019. https://time.com/magazine/us/4793878/june-5th-2017-vol-189-no-21-u-s/.

Sonneville, K. R., I. B. Thurston, C. E. Milliren, H. C. Gooding, and T. K. Richmond. 2016. "Weight Misperception Among Young Adults with Overweight/Obesity Associated with Disordered Eating Behaviors." *International Journal of Eating Disorders* 49: 937–946.

Spoor, S. T. P., M. H. J. Bekker, T. Van Strien, and G. L. van Heck. 2007. "Relations Between Negative Affect, Coping, and Emotional Eating." *Appetite* 48: 368–376.

Stice, E., K. Davis, N. P. Miller, and C. N. Marti. 2008. "Fasting Increases Risk for Onset of Binge Eating and Bulimic Pathology: A 5-Year Prospective Study." *Journal of Abnormal Psychology* 117: 941–946.

Stice, E., K. Presnell, and D. Spangler. 2002. "Risk Factors for Binge Eating Onset in Adolescent Girls: A 2-Year Prospective Investigation." *Health Psychology* 21: 131–138.

Stone, L. 2009. "Beyond Simple Multi-Tasking: Continuous Partial Attention." *The Attention Project* (blog). November 30. https://lindastone.net/2009/11/30/beyond-simple-multi-tasking-continuous-partial-attention/.

Strecher, V. J., G. H. Seijts, G. J. Kok, G. P. Latham, R. Glasgow, B. DeVellis, R. M. Meertens, and D. W. Bulger. 1995. "Goal Setting as a Strategy for Health Behavior Change." *Health Education Quarterly* 22: 190–200.

Svaldi, J., B. Tuschen-Caffier, P. Peyk, and J. Blechert. 2010. "Information Processing of Food Pictures in Binge Eating Disorder." *Appetite* 55: 685–694.

Svaldi, J., D. Caffier, and B. Tuschen-Caffier. 2010. "Emotion Suppression but Not Reappraisal Increases Desire to Binge in Women with Binge Eating Disorder." *Psychotherapy and Psychosomatics* 79: 188–190.

Swanson, S. A., S. J. Crow, D. Le Grange, J. Swendsen, and K. R. Merikangas. 2011. "Prevalence and Correlates of Eating Disorders in Adolescents." *Archives of General Psychiatry* 68: 714–723.

Tomiyama, A. J. 2014. "Weight Stigma Is Stressful: A Review of Evidence for the Cyclic Obesity/Weight-Based Stigma Model." *Appetite* 82: 8–15.

Tomiyama, A. J., T. Mann, D. Vinas, J. M. Hunger, J. Dejager, and S. E. Taylor. 2010. "Low Calorie Dieting Increases Cortisol." *Psychosomatic Medicine* 72: 357–364.

Tribole, E., and E. Resch. 2017. *The Intuitive Eating Workbook: Ten Principles for Nourishing a Healthy Relationship with Food.* Oakland, CA: New Harbinger.

Troisi, J., S. Gabriel, J. Derrick, and A. Geisler. 2015. "Threatened Belonging and Preference for Comfort Food Among the Securely Attached." *Appetite* 90: 58–64.

Vocks, S., B. Tuschen-Caffier, R. Pietrowsky, S. J. Rustenbach, A. Kersting, and S. Herpertz. 2010. "Meta-Analysis of the Effectiveness of Psychological and Pharmacological Treatments for Binge Eating Disorder." *International Journal of Eating Disorders* 43: 205–217.

Waldinger, R. J., S. Cohen, M. S. Schulz, and J. A. Crowell. 2015. "Security of Attachment to spouses in Late Life: Concurrent and Prospective Links with Cognitive and emotional Wellbeing." *Clinical Psychological Science* 3: 516–529.

Walker, M. 2017. *Why We Sleep.* New York: Simon & Schuster, Inc.

Warren, J. M., N. Smith, and M. Ashwell. 2017. "A Structured Literature Review on the Role of Mindfulness, Mindful Eating and Intuitive Eating in Changing Eating Behaviors: Effectiveness and Associated Potential Mechanisms." *Nutrition Research Reviews* Dec. 30: 272–383.

Wegner, D. 1997. "When the Antidote Is the Poison: Ironic Mental Control Processes." *Psychological Science* 8: 148–150.

Wegner, D. M., D. J. Schneider, S. R. Carter III, and T. L. White. 1987. "Paradoxical Effects of Thought Suppression." *Journal of Personality and Social Psychology* 53: 5–13.

Weissman, M., J. Markowitz, and G. Klerman. 2007. *Clinician's Quick Guide to Interpersonal Psychotherapy.* New York: Oxford University Press, Inc.

Wells, J., S. Hobfoll, and J. Lavin. 1999. "When It Rains, It Pours: The Greater Impact of Resource Loss Compared to Gain on Psychological Distress." *Personality and Social Psychology Bulletin* 25: 1,172–1,182.

Wing, R., and S. Phelan. 2005. "Long-Term Weight Loss Maintenance." *American Journal of Clinical Nutrition* 82: 222–225.

Womble, L. G., D. A. Williamson, C. K. Martin, N. L. Zucker, J. M. Thaw, R. Netemeyer, J. C. Lovejoy, and F. L. Greenway. 2001. "Psychosocial Variables Associated with Binge Eating in Obese Males and Females." *International Journal of Eating Disorders* 30: 217–221.

Yalom, I. 2009. *Staring at the Sun.* San Francisco: Jossey-Bass.

Zeeck, A., N. Stelzer, H. W. Linster, A. Joos, and A. Hartmann. 2011. "Emotion and Eating in Binge Eating Disorder and Obesity." *European Eating Disorders Review* 19: 426–437.

Gia Marson, EdD, is a licensed psychologist with private practices in Santa Monica and Malibu, CA. Marson is the psychologist consultant to the University of California, Los Angeles (UCLA) Adolescent and Young Adult Medicine Nourish for Life eating disorders program. She is also an integrative health coach trained by Duke Integrative Medicine, and serves as clinical director for the Breaking The Chains Foundation. Marson has spent the last two decades helping clients reach their whole health goals by conducting trainings, teaching, and providing clinical supervision. She also served as director of the UCLA CAPS Eating Disorder Program, a psychologist on the UCLA Athletic Care Committee, and as a clinician at The Renfrew Center's Intensive Outpatient Program, and the Monte Nido Treatment Center's Residential Program.

Danielle Keenan-Miller, PhD, is a psychological scientist, teacher, and therapist. She is director of the UCLA Psychology Clinic, and associate adjunct professor of psychology at UCLA where she trains graduate students in evidence-based psychotherapy. She has written more than a dozen scientific articles, and serves on the board of the Association of Psychology Training Clinics. Along with Marson, she is cofounder of www.psychologistsecrets.com. She also has a private practice in Los Angeles, CA, where she blends the art and science of psychotherapy.

MORE BOOKS *from*
NEW HARBINGER PUBLICATIONS

A MINDFULNESS-BASED STRESS REDUCTION WORKBOOK, SECOND EDITION

978-16840-3553 / US $25.95

THE UPWARD SPIRAL

Using Neuroscience to Reverse the Course of Depression, One Small Change at a Time

978-1626251205 / US $18.95

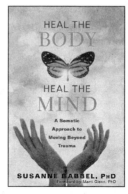

HEAL THE BODY, HEAL THE MIND

A Somatic Approach to Moving Beyond Trauma

978-1684031047 / US $16.95

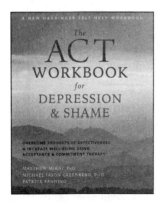

THE ACT WORKBOOK FOR DEPRESSION & SHAME

Overcome Thoughts of Defectiveness and Increase Well-Being Using Acceptance & Commitment Therapy

978-1684035540 / US $22.95

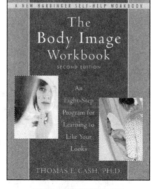

THE BODY IMAGE WORKBOOK, SECOND EDITION

An Eight-Step Program for Learning to Like Your Looks

978-1572245464 / US $25.95

SHOW YOUR ANXIETY WHO'S BOSS

A Three-Step CBT Program to Help You Reduce Anxious Thoughts & Worry

978-1684034055 / US $16.95

newharbingerpublications
1-800-748-6273 / newharbinger.com

(VISA, MC, AMEX / prices subject to change without notice)

Follow Us 🅞 🅕 🅨 ▶ 🅟 in

Don't miss out on new books in the subjects that interest you.
Sign up for our **Book Alerts** at **newharbinger.com/bookalerts**

Register your **new harbinger** titles for additional benefits!

When you register your **new harbinger** title—purchased in any format, from any source—you get access to benefits like the following:

- Downloadable accessories like printable worksheets and extra content

- Instructional videos and audio files

- Information about updates, corrections, and new editions

Not every title has accessories, but we're adding new material all the time.

Access free accessories in 3 easy steps:

1. Sign in at NewHarbinger.com (or **register** to create an account).

2. Click on **register a book**. Search for your title and click the **register** button when it appears.

3. Click on the **book cover or title** to go to its details page. Click on **accessories** to view and access files.

That's all there is to it!

If you need help, visit:

NewHarbinger.com/accessories

new harbinger
CELEBRATING
40 YEARS